MW00942189

GET IN THE BOAT

Inside an Impossible Boat with a Possible God

A Journey of Infertility and Adoption with

Jesus as Our Captain

SHEENA ROCK

ISBN 978-1-0980-0161-2 (paperback)
ISBN 978-1-0980-0163-6 (digital)

Christian Faith Publishing, Inc.
832 Park Avenue
Meadville, PA 16335
www.christianfaithpublishing.com

Printed in the United States of America

That day when evening came, he said to his disciples, "Let us go over to the other side." Leaving the crowd behind, they took him along, just as he was, in the boat. There were also other boats with him. A furious squall came up, and the waves broke over the boat, so that it was nearly swamped. Jesus was in the stern, sleeping on a cushion. The disciples woke him and said to him, "Teacher, don't you care if we drown?" He got up, rebuked the wind and said to the waves, "Quiet! Be still!" Then the wind died down and it was completely calm. He said to his disciples, "Why are you so afraid? Do you still have no faith?" They were terrified and asked each other, "Who is this? Even the wind and the waves obey him!" (Mark 4:35–41)

Have you ever been asked by Jesus to get into a boat and go to the other side, and not only to go to the other side, but end up in one whale of a storm along the way? I came across this New Testament story, and as often happens when I read a passage in the Bible, I received a new, refreshing take on the text. Although I have read it many times before and have heard it many times used in a Sunday sermon, this time, the Holy Spirit gave me a new sense of understanding. Before, I had always read it in a more literal manner; however, this time, I started to understand it and look at it in a figurative way, realizing there have been multiple times in my life where Jesus has asked me to climb into a boat. One of the most life-changing sailing experiences I have had with Jesus was when He asked me to get into an adoption cruise liner.

With two failed miscarriages, my husband, Nathan, and I began to question what God's will was for our lives. As with the story above, this adoption "boat" has not come without storms—storms that have made us question God and our purpose. Our prayer is that through the pages of this book, you will be able to find comfort and hope in our God story. The one thing Nate and I are determined to do is to use the miscarriages and the adoption process for the good and glory of God's kingdom. I wanted to write this book as a way to glorify God and get this story of one of His answered miracles out there, so that the world will know and believe that God is still in control and still in the process of granting miracles. For the purposes of confidentiality and discretion, I have changed some of the names and places in our story.

My sincere desire is that our story will bring you growth and a renewed hope. This journey at times has really tested our faith. At times, we just broke down with intense sadness, grief, and disappointment, but God taught us to grow, lean, and trust in Him. I have included my actual journal entries in the upcoming pages, a true look into my deepest and innermost thoughts. It is my sincere prayer that the God of all comfort, the ultimate healer, and our Father above will give you immense encouragement as you read the following pages, whatever your story may be or wherever you are in your walk with Jesus, and that the God of the universe will reveal His will for your life.

I do want to add a personal disclaimer here by saying that these are my viewpoints and opinions. By no means should anything in this book be considered legal or professional counsel, as there is no way to fully understand each scenario or personal struggle of those that read this book. God bless.

Sheena

CHAPTER 1

Getting into the Boat

That day when evening came, he said to
his disciples, "Let us go over to the other
side." Leaving the crowd behind, they took
him along, just as he was, in the boat.
There were also other boats with him.
—Mark 4:35–36

On the eve of Thanksgiving in 2014, Nathan and I had just gotten
home from visiting with my grandmother when we found out we
were expecting our first child. We stopped at the local pharmacy prior
to going to my grandmother's house, as we knew there was a chance
we were pregnant. At that time, I had been about four days late,
which was very odd for me. We decided beforehand that we would
wait until after the visit before taking the pregnancy test because we
knew if we had received a positive test beforehand, we would not
have been able to truly visit with my grandmother in respect to the
overwhelming excitement, so as soon as we got home, I took that
test. Now, when we went to the store to buy the test, it was the first
test we had ever taken, so we really didn't know what to look for.

There were several types of tests, but we decided to buy the one
that would come up with the clearest answer we could imagine—
flashing either "pregnant" or "not pregnant." Sitting on the edge
of the bed, I remember thinking, *What if we are actually pregnant?*

The timer went off. It was time to check. I made Nate look at it first. I was literally shaking with fear, excitement, and whatever else I could possibly feel. He got off the bed, walked over to the bathroom sink, and picked up the applicator. He came out of the bathroom. I had gotten up at that time and walked halfway down the hallway, almost to where the bathroom entrance had been. He was holding the applicator, smiling and shaking his head yes. I remember saying, "Seriously?" He just shook his head as tears were rolling down his cheeks and hugged me so tight. I cannot even remember if I hugged him back. I think I did, but I was just in disbelief, totally surprised at the realization of how quick life can totally change—literally in an instant.

Nathan and I had the conversation a few times about whether we wanted to have a child, and every time we had the conversation, we never really did decide what to do. You see, we were so happy being together that we weren't sure we were meant to be more than a two-person family, only ever to hear, "Rock. Party of two." At the end of one of our conversations, we decided that we would stop trying to plan our own lives and let God take control of the situation, getting rid of all contraceptives that we had, and letting God take the wheel. Looking back, we did what was right by giving God control of the situation, but I don't remember us really praying or fasting over it when we should have been. We should have been drawing closer to God in these ways and seeking His wisdom and discernment.

Now the next day was Thanksgiving, and we just learned this incredible truth. There was no way we were going to be able to keep this a secret. If you know my husband, you would know this to be a definite truth. We have heard people say that you shouldn't tell anyone about your pregnancy until you reach the six-week mark or the nine-week mark. We tossed that advice out the window. We have heard of others having miscarriages, but this wasn't anything that would or could happen to us, or at least we thought that at the time, so we were not concerned at all about sharing our news. Words cannot even express the feelings and emotions we had. I remember we would just look at each other and smile, knowing we had this incredible secret and new gift from God.

Thanksgiving Day came, and boy did we have a lot to be thankful for. We went to Nathan's grandmother's house first for dinner, which was the normal holiday routine. Nathan's mother, father, sister, brother-in-law, and great-aunt would also be assembled at the table. Nathan kept looking over at me, smiling. I knew he was secretly asking me if I was ready to tell, and I would shake my head ever so slightly no. I was so nervous and afraid of what their opinions about it would be. Nate and I had only been married for about four months at the time, and as you will see later in the story, our history was a bit of a rocky one to say the least. I had had to re-earn the approval of Nathan's family, and so I wasn't ready to face the reality of whether or not that was going to change again. We ended up deciding not to tell them and headed over to my parents' house for dinner number two. My parents only live about a stone's throw away from Nathan's grandparents. Actually, Nathan's parents' house and his great-aunt's house are also located within a two-block radius. To say this was small-town living was an understatement. Over at my parent's house, my sister, her son, and his girlfriend were already there, awaiting our arrival to begin the turkey feast.

I had a little bit of a headache and asked my mother if she had any low strength Tylenol. She said she had something else (I cannot even remember what the name of the brand was now), but I said, "Well, I'm not sure I can take that," and then it just came out, "because I'm pregnant." My mother's eyes got huge and she said, "Seriously?" Then she just hugged me and made Nate and me run downstairs to where my dad was in the basement, his man cave. He started crying and hugged us both so tightly. I told Nate, "Well, we have to go back over to your Gram's house now to tell your family." And I say Nate was bad with secrets. We drove the two minutes back over to tell Nathan's family.

As we opened the sliding glass door that gave us entry into Rosie's (Nate's Gram's) house, everyone gave us a strange look, trying to figure out what in the world we were doing. As we told his family, everyone was speechless from total surprise and excitement. We got hugs from all around.

Fast-forward about four weeks. I had the pregnancy glow and all the morning sickness I could handle. Once, I was sitting at work and couldn't determine if I was going to throw up or pass out. We had our first gynecological appointment made and were looking forward to it. When the day finally came, we entered the gynecological office with great anticipation of possibly getting to see the little one on the ultrasound. It was now winter, and we were bundled from head to toe, sitting in those uncomfortable waiting room chairs. I picked up a magazine on what to expect during delivery and started reading the issue. I quickly put that issue back down as soon as I saw a life-size diagram depicting the size of a fully dilated cervix. Nate's eyes were as wide as mine.

Moments later, we were called back into a private office where we went through the hour-long questionnaire of our personal and family histories. We were then escorted to the exam room where my nurse midwife entered about twenty minutes later. She said that since I was only about nine weeks, she would skip the cervical exam and take me to get the ultrasound. Honestly, it was almost lunch time, so I believe she was just trying to move a little quicker through my exam to get me moving out the door faster. Either way, we didn't fuss.

The ultrasound was the part that we were excited about anyway. I got situated on the exam table, and she started the ultrasound. After searching for a few minutes, she asked me, "Did I ever tell you on any of your prior PAP smears and cervical exams that you had a tilted uterus?" I assured her that she hadn't, and she gave a "hmm" response and said, "Well, maybe it's not a viable pregnancy." Honestly, I had no idea what that meant, and she seemed really calm and unnerved by it, so I just shook that off, not thinking it meant anything serious. She proceeded to tell me to go ahead and get dressed, and she would get me an appointment with the downstairs ultrasound group and that she was having trouble finding the fetus. Nathan and I were confused, anxiousness started to creep in to our thoughts.

They couldn't get us an appointment with the downstairs ultrasound technicians for another two hours; so we went home for a little bit, just prayed, and ate some lunch. We kept telling ourselves everything would be fine and that God had everything under control. Meanwhile, both of our cellular phones were blowing up with our family and friends, texting us for updates on what was going on and how the little one was doing.

Walking through the street in the winter cold, hopping into the elevator, and proceeding to walk to the ultrasound imaging station, there was a definite loss of pep in our step, less air in our lungs, and less excitement than that which we had started the day. We had to wait another twenty to thirty minutes to be called back into a new exam room. I tried occupying my mind by watching *Family Feud,* which was playing on the waiting room television screen, but my thoughts raced only on getting back to that room and seeing our baby. The ultrasound technician performed a transvaginal ultrasound, thinking that I possibly misjudged the length of my pregnancy and that I wasn't quite as far along as I had thought, but she also could not find the heartbeat or the fetus. She stated that she saw a gestational sac that just looked like a black hole and left the room to go get the doctor without explaining why. However, we could tell by the look on her face that something was amiss.

For forty minutes, Nathan and I sat there in a state of fear and of the unknown. We had no idea what was happening. My feet were turning blue from being in that cold room for so long just waiting. Every tick of that clock felt like an hour, and each tick sounded louder and louder. Once the physician finally came in, he introduced himself to us. He was a well-known physician in our community and known for his professional excellence in his field. He also performed the ultrasound for us, and then it happened. He found the baby. I saw it up on the screen at the exact same time that Nathan saw it. It was the most exciting and most beautiful thing I have ever seen. I turned to Nate and said, "Oh…there's the baby," and we both just smiled. Nate had tears in his eyes. Our hope and happiness returned. It looked like a gummy bear on that screen, and so that is what we named our first child, Gummy.

Again though, without missing a beat, the doctor said, "I have sad news for you." Back to earth we came, the smiles leaving our faces, and our hearts dropping again. He then proceeded to give us the gravity of our miscarriage. He said I had two options—I could let the miscarriage happen naturally or have a surgical removal. He informed us that we should have been about nine weeks along according to the dates I had given him, however, the baby seems to have passed at six weeks. He did say that it was just biology and to not beat ourselves up over what had happened and that it didn't happen because of something we did or didn't do. The doctor then proceeded to tell us that we could go out the back door, so that we wouldn't have to go out the front. *Should we be feeling ashamed?* That thought ran through my mind for an instant. The doctor then proceeded to get up out of the chair, wash his hands, and leave the room. The only one throughout the entire day who seemed to have had any bedside manner with us was the new physician who was shadowing at that time. He actually took my hand and said he was sorry for our loss. The remainder of the staff acted as if it was business as usual, just a normal day at the office.

Looking back, I remember about two to three weeks prior to this appointment that I no longer felt any morning sickness and was having some cramping, but since I had never been pregnant before, I really didn't know that this was odd or unnatural. Once throughout the night, I felt a sharper cramp that awoke me from sleep. I thought that maybe the cramping was just gas pains. I did research this on the Internet and read that a little cramping can be normal. My OB office had stated they don't like to see patients before the nine-week mark, so I didn't think anything of this at the time.

Nathan and I were silent on the ride home. We had to call our parents and give them the grave news. However, we still refused to believe it ourselves. We told ourselves that we served a big God who was still in the miracle business. We decided to let the miscarriage happen naturally in case the doctor was wrong, or God chose to grant us a miracle. About two weeks later, the bleeding started, as well as the incredible pain. It was both mentally and physically traumatic and horrifying.

Journal Entry: Tuesday, January 6, 2015
   "Miscarriage Day"
   We had the first baby visit today. Our nurse midwife couldn't find the baby on the ultrasound, so we had to go downstairs and have the ultrasound techs take a look.

   The tech said she saw a gestational sac that just looked like a black hole and then said she had to go find the doctor. He came back and was able to find the baby, but it was only six weeks old, meaning the baby stopped growing about three weeks ago.

   I'll never forget seeing the baby on the screen, so happy they found him/her. I now have the options of having a D&C or passing the baby myself.

   Receiving lots of love from family and friends but finding I just want to be alone.

Journal Entry: Wednesday, January 7, 2015
   "Denial"
   This has been an extremely rough day. I find I am scared to go to the bathroom for fear of passing the baby. Also, I find I am in denial.

   Heal me, Lord, for my body is in agony. I am sick at heart. How long until you restore me (Ps. 6:2–3)?

   God blesses those who mourn for they will be comforted (Matt. 5:4).

Journal Entry: Friday, January 23, 2015
   The miscarriage started today. Denial is over. God said no.

Journal Entry: February 13, 2015
   Still having problems sleeping. I find I have insomnia. I cannot sleep day or night. My

thoughts are constant. How I wish I could turn them off. It's making me crazy and angry.

Nathan doesn't get it, and he seems to just be able to go about his daily life. I feel like my life has stopped. I miss Gummy!

The pain continued, but the bleeding stopped, and about a month later, I was late again. I took a pregnancy test, and it showed once again that I was pregnant. Nathan was away on business during that week, and I didn't want him to worry so far away from home, so I chose not to tell him anything over the phone. I went and got blood work to have my PSA levels checked, and it was showing I was pregnant as well. I decided that maybe this would be a nice surprise for him and exactly what we needed to get over the loss, so I decided to wrap the pregnancy test up as a gift for him to open. When Nathan got home that Thursday from his work trip, I gave him the gift. He opened it, cocked his head, and gave me a confused look. I went on to explain what had transpired over the past week. He wasn't excited or emotional at all. I was looking right at a blank canvas of nothing on his face.

That following day, which was a Friday, I began having more intense, abdominal pain that doubled me over. I couldn't get out of bed as the pain became so great. I called the OB office and had the hardest time even getting an appointment. They tried telling me to just take Tylenol and that they would try to get me in the following week for an appointment. My husband and I would not accept that answer. The pain was too great. I had to fight over the phone with them to get any sort of treatment. After hours (literally hours) of phone calls, begging and pleading for someone to do something, they finally set me up for a same day ultrasound. This ultrasound showed that I had not been pregnant again but that I just hadn't fully miscarried Gummy. Gratefully, they performed some schedule changes in order to get me set up for a D&C (dilation and curettage) the following Monday, three days away. I stayed in bed that entire weekend, trying to find some type of position that would help the pain or give me some type of relief.

The day of the D&C, I had this amazing nurse, which Nathan and I both agree was a gift from God. She spoke like she was from deeper south, like New Orleans, and I just appreciated her so much. She saw on my chart what I was in for, and she said she was extremely sorry for our loss. It was just nice to have someone say that and recognize that it was a loss that we suffered. I had a deep appreciation for this genuine woman and the compassion she showed to me and how God places gems along our paths. We just have to keep our eyes open and look for them.

After awakening from the procedure, they wheeled me back to my outpatient recovery room where Nathan was waiting. I felt the loss at that time and knew that it was over; a major wave of emptiness was taking root down to the core of my soul. With tears in my eyes, I looked over at Nate. He grabbed my hand. "I don't want to try again, okay?" That was the first thing I said to him. He gave me the most compassionate look and said whatever I wanted to do would be fine with him, and he never wanted to see me go through this much pain ever again.

I remained in a state of sadness for weeks after. During a D&C, a thin instrument is inserted into the uterus, and it is used to remove tissue from the inside of the uterus. Having someone literally scrapping your baby out of you is just horrendous to think about and to deal with. I remember thinking things like, *Did they just throw my baby away? Should I have asked for it?* The thousands of thoughts that went through my mind felt debilitating and left me feeling disgusting. Depressive thoughts against myself were also getting harder and harder to fight off. I started finding every way to blame myself.

For months following this, Nathan and I just prayed asking God's guidance on what He wanted us to do. Should we try again to have a baby naturally (even though neither one of us wanted this to be an option at this point), or should we try to adopt, or should we just be Aunt Sheen and Uncle Nate and perhaps find a different will from God? We thought perhaps God didn't want us to have children of our own at all and that maybe we were meant for missions or something else altogether. This was one of the times where we felt that Jesus was asleep on our boat. We felt like we couldn't get any type of answer or guidance from Him. He was just silent while the waves continued crashing into us, thrusting us back down anytime we felt we were gaining some sort of ground or regaining our breaths.

This continued for months until one Sunday morning. I was talking to God in the car on the way to church. To myself, I prayed, *Okay, God. If you want me and Nate to do something, you are going to have to let it hit us square in the forehead because I am just not getting it, nor do I feel we have an answer to this question that we have asked you for over and over.* Now this Sunday was no ordinary Sunday and was already going to be tough. It was Mother's Day—the first Mother's Day since I had found out I was pregnant and had the miscarriage. I woke up an emotional mess and questioned whether I should even try going to church at all, but I fought against those thoughts. Where better to be than in the house of the Lord, the ultimate Healer?

Well, our Pastor that morning preached on James 1:27, "Religion that God our Father accepts as pure and faultless is this: to look after orphans and widows in their distress and to keep oneself from being polluted by the world." That was it! God had spoken right to me and hit me right in the forehead like I asked. He wanted us to adopt and care for His orphaned children. We left church, and I didn't want to say anything to Nathan to see if he would bring it up. I wanted to see if he had felt God speaking to him in this manner. He didn't say anything, so after a while, I finally asked him what he thought of the service and whether he felt God had spoken to his heart about anything. He smiled slightly and said, "Yes. I heard it too. I think God is moving for us to adopt a child. Now I need to go buy a tree and do some landscaping or something because otherwise, I am going to explode." We both just started laughing and crying at the same time. We were both scared out of our minds and yet extremely relieved to have gotten an answer. By the way, we did drive to a local nursery to buy some plants, went home, and did do some landscaping that day.

Even after this answer, Nathan had a challenging time getting on the boat. He was struggling with the fact that the child would not be ours in the natural sense. We grew up in small town USA where what you did after high school was go to college, get married, buy a home next to your parents in the same school district you graduated from, and start your own family; wash, rinse, repeat. Nobody on Nathan's side of the family had ever adopted, and the endless possibilities of what this looked like was difficult for him to swallow.

To go further with our story, I think it is time to give you a background of us.

CHAPTER 2

In the beginning, God…

The first four words in the Bible are "In the beginning God" (Gen. 1:1). Well, those are the same four words that begin the story of Nathan and I's relationship.

Growing up, Nathan and I attended grade school through high school together. We became neighbors in the summer before seventh grade when my parents moved into a house that came up for sale about a quarter of a mile away from Nathan's parents. We began to ride the same school bus, having the same bus stop. Dating back even further, my father and Nathan's father attended high school together, played on the high school football team together, and they even shared the same birth date. Nathan and I were close growing up, and in about ninth grade, we started officially dating, or as much as you can officially date in the ninth grade.

There was a small hill in between our parents' houses, and that is where we used to meet. We cleverly called it The Hill. Back then, we didn't have cellular phones. We had landlines, so we would also find ways of communicating this way. I remember turning down shopping with my aunt numerous times so that I would be home just in case Nathan would call. I didn't want to miss it. Nathan's curfews were a lot earlier than mine and were strictly enforced by his mother. My curfew was much later, and even then, I really don't remember it being enforced that much. Of course, I never stayed out past my curfew to find out. I am a "by the book" kind of gal. I believe in coloring in the lines and following all the rules to a "T." Nathan is not this way. I remember there were times when his mother would send his sister up to the hill to scold him that it was time to get his butt home, reminding him it was past curfew.

I hated that Nathan had this curfew. I loved spending time with him, and the time we had never seemed to be enough. Nathan is the most amazing person. Growing up, I thought he was perfect. He had the perfect family, was an All-American athlete in football, basketball, track, and anything else he tried out for. On top of that, he is extremely intelligent—one of those guys that can multiply large numbers in his head and can recall stats at the drop of a hat, barely even batting an eye. Everyone liked and likes Nathan. I cannot remember a single person that didn't, and as a matter of fact, Nathan ended up being our Homecoming King and Mr. Senior our senior year, class of 2001.

I was more standoffish and an introvert. Although popularity came naturally to me all the way up to and throughout junior high, I started struggling with anxiety around tenth grade. Things that I had bore witness to in my past and throughout my childhood caught up with me in what felt like an instant, all leading to a mental exhaustion full of anxiousness, timidity, and unnatural fears that I allowed to take over my life.

I was always a shy person, but I began to withdraw completely. I stopped hanging out socially with friends and attending high school events. Even if I would attend, I wouldn't enjoy them. As I previously stated, I was extremely timid all the time, suffering from extreme anxiety, which I allowed to start making me sick and affect me physically. This, in turn, spiraled into missing a load of school. At the end of every school year, I missed the maximum amount of days possible before having to repeat the grade. Looking back now, I think about how sad it was that nobody around me or from the school system seemed to even care or take notice of these warning signs. As long as I turned in my absentee excuse on time, there were never any questions raised.

During phone conversations or our time on the hill, I tried talking to Nathan about things that were going on, but unless you have dealt with the things I was dealing with, it's hard to grasp. On top of that, I was embarrassed and kept a lot of things hidden. The few times I visited Nathan's childhood home, I struggled. I felt so out of place there and not because his family made me feel that way. On the contrary, they made me feel very welcome. It was just that I couldn't relate to this type of environment. I was a fish out of water here, and truthfully, I was incredibly jealous. This was the life I wanted to have. I wanted normalcy and a sense of safety and security. I stopped going over to visit his family because I told myself I didn't belong there amongst them, and I honestly believed that. I believed that I was dirty somehow or marked. I began to realize that I loved Nathan too much to allow him to be brought down into my madness. He just had so much going for him, and I didn't want to compromise that or his life in any way, so in tenth grade, I called it quits on our relationship.

I know that doesn't seem like a big deal, but to us, it was. You see, we knew, even at sixteen, that we were soul mates. I don't know how else to explain it other than to say that we just knew we had a bond. There was some deeply rooted connection there. He tried not to listen to me and ignore my breakup with him. But one day, I had to have a heart to heart with him about it all, how I was feeling, and why I was making the decision that I was making. I even said that I honestly felt we would end up back together someday, but it just wasn't our time right now. I could tell that he still couldn't understand. The things that I explained to him were bothersome to me and causing me great mental anguish in life seemed "cool" to him. He didn't get the severity of the imprints it was leaving in my life, so he continued to ignore the breakup and continued to believe we were still an item.

Inevitably, I just stopped talking to him and taking his phone calls. I pulled away from a lot of our mutual friends and started hanging out with people who seemed to have lives more like mine. I liked that I didn't have to hide who I was around these new friends as they had issues going on, too, and no one cared that we had them. That's where I met my ex-husband. To me, he was exactly what I needed. He was strong, both mentally and physically, never caring what others thought, and because of this, he would gladly raise his voice to anyone who did me an injustice. Being timid, this was not something I did or felt I could do for myself, so this made me feel so secure and safe. He had the ability to take me away from situations I didn't need or want to be in, and although I knew he wasn't necessarily my soul mate, I believed that this was the person I needed to be with—the one that could take me away from the small town that I never felt I fit into, to take me away from all of the chaos that was weighing me down and keeping me from flight.

We dated the remainder of high school, and the moment that I graduated, I found an apartment and moved out from under my parents' roof. Not long after, my ex-husband, who was still my boyfriend at the time, moved in with me. As you can see, God's will for my life was far from my thoughts and actions. I rarely gave God any serious thought, let alone what He wanted for my life. A few months later, my parents experienced a house fire. It was a total loss of everything. They had to tear down and rebuild, and the small town was right there behind them. I give small towns a bad rap, but they are fantastic at being caring and loving communities. Included in that help was Nathan and his family.

I hadn't seen Nathan since we graduated, so it was really nice to see him. Both Nathan and his father spent many hours at my parents' house, helping them to rebuild. Once, I happened to be there at the same time. I was alone, and Nathan asked me if I would be willing to go for a drive with him saying that there was something he needed to speak to me about. I decided to go, feeling both reluctance and yearning, reluctance because I knew this would not bode well with my ex but also yearning because it had been years since I spoke with Nate, and I really wanted to just be in his presence.

So, one evening, we got into his silver Dodge Shadow and just drove all around the back roads of our small town. This was something he enjoyed doing, but to me, it just reminded me of how small this town really was and just how bad I wanted to be rid of it. I asked him what he wanted to say to me, and it was what I had both hoped and feared. He said that he had just broken up with his girlfriend. He told her he still had feelings for me and wondered if I had the same.

I cannot honestly remember what my response to him was, but I can say for certain what I remember feeling. I was excited and hopeful, something I hadn't felt in a long time. I wanted to tell him the truth, that there was nothing I wanted to do more than to give us another try. I wanted to hug him and stay there for hours, just feeling his warmth and taking in his scent. But, I held back. I couldn't go this way with him again. I knew where it would end. If I went back with him now, we would end up getting married, moving to a place near both his and my parents, and I would be stuck forever in this life and this small-town living that I just could not bear. It sickened me to have to hold back, but I did it. I didn't think I could be happy living here, and I knew he couldn't be happy not.

I was also afraid that nothing would have changed, that he still would not be able to grasp the depths of the anxiety and emotions that I felt, nor be able to deal with them in the way that I needed. I also still held true to my tenth grade beliefs. I wanted better for Nathan than what I could give him. I wanted him to have the best that he deserved, and I thought there was no way that could happen with me. I felt that I would be nothing more than a nuisance to him and always holding him back from living his best life. Looking back, I know that it was God pushing me to be with Nathan again, but sadly, I fought against Him. I thought I knew exactly what I needed, and so, I continued on the pathway that I thought was right. In the end, I turned his offer down and again broke his and my hearts. This was the last that we saw each other for about seven years.

I continued dating and living together with my ex throughout college. I got my first job in the spring of 2003. I struggled through it though. My anxiety was at an all-time high, and it continued making me physically ill. I got to the point where I wouldn't even eat unless I was at home because it would make me immensely sick. I went to doctor after doctor trying to figure out what was wrong, and each one kept telling me that I was an incredibly stressed-out individual and that I was the one making myself physically ill. They tried putting me on antianxiety and antidepressant medications, but I hated them. I felt that they made me an empty shell and that I wasn't myself at all.

One day during work, two of my fellow coworkers began talking about church and the Bible. They were speaking about the book of Revelation and how it states that when the end times come, those that were followers of Jesus will be taken up in the rapture, and those that weren't would be left behind. They went on to talk more, and they had my full attention now. They said things regarding the mark of the beast and about salvation. I had gone to church off and on throughout my life, and I couldn't remember a time that this was ever taught to me. The one girl brought me in a Bible, and I gave my life to Jesus in November of 2003.

Not long after that, my boyfriend at the time asked me if I would marry him, and I said yes, but I didn't feel the excitement that should be felt when this question is asked. The funny thing is, I knew this wasn't the man I was supposed to marry—the man God had intended for me to wed, but it was what came next, according to society, so that was the path I walked. I still thought of Nathan often. He was rarely far from my thoughts. I couldn't visit my parents' house without passing his parents' house, and every time I passed, I would hope to get a glimpse of him and let my thoughts wonder to what it might be like right now if I hadn't pushed him away like I pushed everyone else. At times, I would miss him so much that I would just break down and cry. My heart actually hurt from missing Nathan and who I was with him. I missed my laughter. He could make me laugh every single day, and I didn't have that anymore. These days, I rarely laughed about anything. Again, with the ability to look back, I know now that this was God pulling me onto the path that I was to be walking, and again, I pushed back.

My ex was feeling wrong about this decision too. Once, after attending a college seminar, he called me and said that he wouldn't be coming home that evening. He said that he was drinking, and a few of his fellow classmates were going to stay behind and get a room for the night. The only issue with that was, the only classmates I could hear in the background of the phone call were that of giggling girls. I called my mother crying, and she said it was time to move back home and get out of this relationship. In no way, shape or form, did I want that to be the answer, and pride definitely played a role here.

I hate being wrong, and I think in some way I knew breaking it off with my ex would be admitting this. So in the fall of 2005, I married the man that God didn't have planned for me. I remember wanting to run out of the church and go find Nathan, but with family and friends gathered in the pews, I thought it too late. Plus, what would Nathan even say? After our last talk, he became so angry with me that he decided he didn't want to talk with me ever again. And, what would his parents say? There were too many what ifs for me to take that risk, so I didn't. What a cool story that would have been, at least for Nathan and me.

Years passed, and my anxiety worsened to where I began to subside into a state of depression. Days when I couldn't get out of bed, my ex felt I was just being lazy and would make some sort of comment to that affect. It had been two years since I had given my life to Christ. I still hadn't given Him full control, but I knew that He was the answer to the healing of my depression, so I started attending church on a more regular basis; and since my ex was not a man of faith, he couldn't understand that either, especially when I wanted to tithe ten percent of our income. The income he reminded me regularly was mostly his. I was having a hard time keeping a job on account of having a high absentee rate. I was allowing the anxiety and depression to overrun my entire life.

It didn't get better either. I started drifting into a really dark place where, sometimes, only a speck of light the size of a freckle could be seen. I know now that was God there with me in that dark place. He was always there. My thoughts began to turn suicidal—never to the extent that I would actually go through with it on account of my faith, but I would think things like, *My family would be better off without me. I need to stop being such a burden to everyone. If I would just go away, everyone could be happier.*

My marriage continued to digress. My ex picked up extra shifts at work just to stay away from our home and from me and stopped even spending my birthdays with me. Finally, the day came when he sat down and just said he was unhappy. We ended up divorcing a few months later. I don't want to portray my ex-husband as a bad person. Actually, my beliefs are on the contrary. He is a very respectable man, and for the years that he was there for me and got me out of some undesirable situations, I owe a gratitude of debt and will be forever grateful.

As I had only been working part-time, I didn't have the finances to buy him out of our house, so I had to pick up and move the thirty-some miles back home. I had to leave a job that I loved and was actually able to hold on to, my church, and my home; going back to that town that I thought I would never have to live in again. Let's just say the depression didn't get any better with this new situation. I asked God why He would let this happen, especially since I had just given my life back to Him. Why did I have to lose everything I had worked for in my life?

Awhile later, I privately messaged Nathan on his social media account, and let's just say the rest is history. He had been living in Pittsburgh and had never married. He tells me now that he knew the moment he saw that message on social media, that that was it and that we were going to be together forever from here on out. He said that the heart he had hardened toward me melted.

My message to him was just casual. I asked him how he was doing and updated him on how my family was. I didn't tell him I was divorced. That was not a road that I wanted to go down at that time. As a matter of fact, I vowed to myself that I was never going to remarry and that I would never allow myself ever again to get under someone so much that I would have to uproot my whole life when the relationship ended. However, small towns being what they are, word got out. One night, Nathan's dad asked him if he knew why my car was at my parents' house so much. Now, there is no doubt that he already knew, but he wanted to hear it from Nate. It was at that time that Nate decided to tell them that we had been back in touch with each other. On a side note, we actually call Nate's dad, the mayor, because he seriously knows everyone and everything that goes on.

We decided it was time to at least meet, so one night, we did. There was nowhere we felt we could go, as we really didn't want word getting out that we were hanging out together, nor did we want rumors to get started, so we decided to just drive around back roads. We literally drove around for six hours! We laughed because I told him that with all the driving we did, we could have been to Ocean City, Maryland, by now. We talked about everything too, and it just felt so good to laugh again.

We continued texting back and forth after this, and one day, Nathan asked me if I would meet him in Pittsburgh to go see a movie. It was a weekday, but I decided to go. I needed to be out of the house to keep the four walls from closing in on me. He gave me directions to his apartment, and I met him there. We made sure his roommate didn't see me as he also was a former high school colleague who still had a lot of connections back home, so we thought it best to keep him in the dark.

At the movies that night, Nathan maintained keeping a distance, but I decided to close that, at least a little. I curled up in my seat and laid my head on his shoulder, taking in his familiar scent. His warmth radiated throughout my entire body, and it just felt right to be that close. It felt like the universe made sense again. After the movie, we drove back to Nathan's apartment. He pulled up next to where my car was parked, and I thanked him for the wonderful night out. We hugged, and as I was pulling away from that hug, Nathan grabbed my head and pulled me in to kiss me. I knew what I had promised myself in regard to starting another relationship, but for this, I could not find the strength to pull away.

God allowed Nathan and I the opportunity to share two first kisses. This was one. The other one was when we were sixteen and standing on top of the hill. Nathan's curfew time was up, and I could tell he wanted to kiss me. It had been like this the past couple of times we had met up, but Nathan never made the first move, and I was way to shy at that time to initiate it. This time seemed to be the same. We said goodbye and turned our back to each other, heading in the opposite directions toward home. All of a sudden, Nathan said something. I think it was something like hold on or I'm going for it, or something to that extent. I turned around to see what he was saying, and before I could make sense of the situation, he was right in front of my face, kissing me, and then every time I tried to turn away to go back home, he would say, "Wait. Just one more." I smiled the entire way home with a grin so wide it must have covered my entire face. I believe Nate did as well, but I also think Nate was in big trouble for missing curfew, again.

The same thing happened this time too. We kept saying just one more kiss, except then, neither one of us would move. Finally, I realized it actually was my move to make as I had to get out of his truck, so after one final kiss, I opened the door and got out, smiling. However, that was short-lived. By the time I made it halfway home, I started crying. *What was I doing? How could I do this? The last thing I need is to get into another relationship, especially with Nathan.*

This back and forth in my mind went on for months. Physically, I just couldn't resist being in Nathan's presence any longer. However, emotionally, I would build walls to keep him out. Nathan has a stubborn quality, which is normally a not-so-attractive feature, but this time it paid off. He said he wasn't ever letting me go again no matter how many walls he had to break down, no matter how long it would take. He was willing to go all in for this chance.

We married in July of 2013 in Exuma Bay, Bahamas. Nathan cried as I walked down the aisle. It was just the two of us, the way it was always meant to be—my best friend and me. Now, here we are, a few short years later with Jesus asking us to get in the adoption boat and set sail with faith being our compass. We had no reason to get into the boat other than faith, especially whenever we counted the risks and costs. Not only did we not have anywhere close to what we needed to pay for an adoption, but we also had no idea where to start looking or what to do. However, Nate and I surrendered to Jesus and got into the boat. We loved Jesus and wanted to follow Him.

While in this part of the journey, of just getting into the boat, God taught us to really look at where we were placing our faith. When Nathan and I began to take a microscopic look at our faith, we realized just how small it really was—nowhere close to that of a mustard seed. We placed our thoughts on the here and now—the financial struggles of an adoption process, the possibility of a foreign placement where we may have to walk into a place with extreme poverty and disease, the agony of a home study and the paperwork processes, and etc. All we were seeing were the ways in which this thing could possibly fail. Once, when Moses was doubting God, God had to tell Moses to get out of his tent and look up in order to put He and Moses into perspective of one another. He also had to do this with us for us to see how big God really is and just how small we are in comparison.

Psalm 77 states this:

> I cried out to God for help;
> I cried out to God to hear me.
> When I was in distress, I sought the Lord;
> at night I stretched out untiring hands,
> and I would not be comforted.
> I remembered you, God, and I groaned;
> I meditated, and my spirit grew faint.
> You kept my eyes from closing;
> I was too troubled to speak.
> I thought about the former days,
> the years of long ago;
> I remembered my songs in the night.
> My heart meditated and my spirit asked:
> "Will the Lord reject forever?
> Will he never show his favor again?
> Has his unfailing love vanished forever?
> Has his promise failed for all time?
> Has God forgotten to be merciful?
> Has he in anger withheld his compassion?"
> Then I thought, "To this I will appeal:
> the years when the Most High stretched out
> his right hand.
> I will remember the deeds of the Lord;
> yes, I will remember your miracles of long ago.
> I will consider all your works
> and meditate on all your mighty deeds."
> Your ways, God, are holy.
> What god is as great as our God?
> You are the God who performs miracles;
> you display your power among the peoples.

With your mighty arm you redeemed your
people,
the descendants of Jacob and Joseph.
The waters saw you, God,
the waters saw you and writhed;
the very depths were convulsed.
The clouds poured down water,
the heavens resounded with thunder;
your arrows flashed back and forth.
Your thunder was heard in the whirlwind,
your lightning lit up the world;
the earth trembled and quaked.
Your path led through the sea,
your way through the mighty waters,
though your footprints were not seen.
You led your people like a flock
by the hand of Moses and Aaron.

We had to take a close look at who we thought God was. Did we still believe God was the same now as He was in the past? Malachi 3:6 states, "I the Lord do not change." In times of toughness, we did struggle with thoughts about whether God was near, and we questioned His plans. Our spirits grew very faint in these times. We were in distress and sought out God's will for our lives, but we did not feel comforted. We couldn't find the happy couple we were before the miscarriage took place. That's not to say we weren't happy. We were just different now. We had scars as tragedies tend to leave. We started questioning, just as the Psalm 77 does, why God rejected us and why He didn't show us favor in this situation. Was He angry with us and withholding His mercy and compassion to punish us?

Thankfully, this Psalm does not stop at verse 9, and it goes on to urge us to remember that God is the same now as He always was and always will be. We needed to determine if we believed that God was still in the business of performing miracles and doing the impossible. James 1:17 tells us that every good and perfect gift is from above, coming down from the Father of the heavenly lights, who does not change like shifting shadows. Even if we couldn't see Him now and even though He felt distant to us, we started remembering the God of the Bible—the one who helped David defeat Goliath with a stone's throw, the one who freed His people from Egyptian slavery by performing many signs and miracles against Pharaoh and the Egyptian people, parting the Red Sea for the Israelites to cross, and while traveling in the wilderness, supplying manna from heaven and water from a rock for them.

We started to see, really see, that God will act if we will believe and be obedient, but we needed to stop looking at the impossible and the incredible hurdles that we were going to face and start looking at the God of the Bible, who says all things are possible with Him. God loves to find unachievable and unattainable goals where only His help makes them achievable and attainable. In this way, His glory and might can be displayed. We started to look up literally and figuratively. Sometimes, I would go outside and look up at the sky. Sometimes, this was at night, while other times, it was day, but it really is something how looking up put me and God in perspective to one another.

This wasn't a onetime thing either. There were many days where I had to come back to this Psalm and re-recite who God is and re-recite His miracles of long ago. Along this path, God placed a special couple into our lives. Friends of ours, who knew we were starting the adoption process, forwarded us a video one day of a couple that had successfully adopted multiple children from Ethiopia. They attended the same high school as Nathan and me, so we knew them quite well. After high school, they got married and began to try and have children of their own—a lot like Nathan and me. After countless miscarriages, God started to guide them toward the route of adoption.

They too were concerned about the financial, travel, and all the other adoption aspects, but they placed their faith in the unknown and began their journey. This journey led them to Ethiopia where they adopted a little boy out of an orphanage there. They had to visit Ethiopia multiple times before being able to actually adopt him, and while they were there, they noticed another family of three that happened to catch their eye. So, a while after adopting their first child, they returned to the orphanage in Ethiopia to adopt those three children. Their video explained how they both could not get those three children out of their minds and how they just knew God was calling them to go back. Later, God would bless them with a child of their own. They went from having no children to now having five.

Their video also explained that they went all in once they knew it was God's calling for them. They began selling off their retirement investments, property, and whatever else they needed to meet the financial aspect. I remember thinking, *Okay, well, I work from home, so we don't need two cars*, and I also had retirement savings that I could cash in. Their story inspired us in so many ways and reminded us that God was going to ask us to be all in, and we needed to be ready for whatever that meant.

It was with extreme pleasure that one day we were able to show them a picture of our baby girl and let them know that their story impacted ours in so many ways. Even after telling them this, I still don't know if they will ever be able to grasp how big their inspiration and contribution was to our own journey.

The passage of Mark above notes that when the disciples got into the boat, they had to leave the crowd behind. This became a huge factor in our own crossing as well. Once we started communicating to our family and friends our wishes to begin the adoption process, we were met with some excited and good reactions, but we were also met with a lot of cynics and skeptics. To those who weren't of Christian faith, this looked extreme and radical, and they weren't sure how to react, especially when we explained the cost and what we were willing to do and to give up to meet this cost.

Some couldn't understand why we wouldn't keep trying to have our own child. Others could not imagine going through the sacrifices needed for us to attain the financial capacity for the adoption, especially when all the monies were going to be nonrefundable and came with no guarantee of a completed adoption. To them this all seemed drastic.

Then, there were those who kept the small-town mentality of having your own children to carry on your own name and legacy. Humorously, what Satan intended to deter us and to place doubts in our minds, is exactly what seemed to confirm God's will for us. The Bible tells us that Jesus is not of this world, and that when you are following God, the world is not going to understand. John 15:19 states, "If you belonged to the world, it would love you as its own. As it is, you do not belong to the world, but I have chosen you out of the world." In John 18:36, Jesus said, "My kingdom is not of this world." We knew that keeping in line with what Jesus wanted us to do would make us feel out of step with the world, and this was being proven by the crowds around us.

Although Nathan and I really craved and wanted the support of our family and friends, before we decided to talk to any of them about our decision, we decided it didn't matter if we had their support or not, that we were going to go through this no matter the consequences. We decided we were going to put God's will for our lives above anything else and trust that He would work everything else out, no matter what this new future might look like. We were going to leave the crowd behind and press on in faith.

The scripture also tells us that the disciples took Jesus along, just as He was. There is no changing God. He is the same now as He was in the past and will be the same in the future, and I am so glad for this. In this world of ever changing circumstances, it's nice to have one constant, especially when that constant is my creator, redeemer, father, and friend. I needed to allow God to work in this situation, no matter what, and allow His timing and perfect will to flow throughout all of it. I needed to step back from the control panel, which is an extremely difficult thing to do for a control addict. Letting go of control tends to allow my anxiety to run amok, but it's truly the only way. We needed to ask Jesus to take the wheel of our boat, just the way He was—perfect.

CHAPTER 3

In the Boat

Although Nathan and I didn't have any family members that had gone through the adoption process, we did know a few friends that had. We started getting the names of the adoption agencies they used and began calling around. It was overwhelming with so many options to choose. There were international adoptions or domestic adoptions. We were asked if we wanted to have an open adoption, a closed adoption, or a semi-open adoption. We were asked what races we would accept and what age groups we would be open to. We needed to choose if we would be interested in fostering children with opportunities to potentially adopt and whether we would be okay with special needs children or children born with drug addictions.

After weeks of research, we had decided to try an international adoption through India. At the time we had been researching, India was, as they called it, the "hot spot," and we could have a child in our home in as little as nine months. Plus, we had a close family friend that had used this particular international adoption agency twice, and both times, they had successful placements. We had also heard nightmarish stories about domestic adoptions. Each state has its own set of laws they follow, and some states allow up to six months for the birth mother to change her mind and take the baby back after adoption. This seemed like an absolute nightmare to us, and we wanted to divert from another possible traumatic experience, so we began the process of an international adoption.

The first thing we needed to do was to get our home study done, but before we even did that, we reached out to our pastor to be on his prayer list. The home study was a rigorous process with a lot of paper work, security background checks, and a home walk through, but we had gotten an amazing caseworker that really helped to make the process easier. As we got deeper in with the adoption agency we were using initially, it became evident that this may not be the agency or the type of adoption God had called us to. I don't know how to quite explain it, but as you may know, when God decides to close a door, it just closes, and you know that it's not the right path anymore. "These are the words of him who is holy and true, who holds the key of David. What he opens no one can shut, and what he shuts no one can open" (Rev. 3:7).

This particular agency was poor about keeping in contact with us or helping us to streamline the process. I remember once, we had a question about how to fill out a certain form they had sent over to us. We called them with this question and even gave them the name of the form. They responded back saying they didn't understand what form we were talking about, which baffled us as they were the ones who sent it on to us in the first place to be filled out, so they had us scan the form back to them in order that they could see what we were talking about. Nathan and I started questioning how comfortable we would be traveling to another country with this agency being our only lifeline of communication back here in the states. On top of that, there was a good chance we wouldn't have access to emails or scanners in the part of the country we would be traveling to. We just felt like God was closing that door. I don't want to say this agency was bad by any means because as I said before, close friends of ours had used this same agency twice with total success. However, we just didn't feel God leading us this way. There seemed to be an awful lot of pushback, and we just felt as if God was closing this door.

Back at the drawing board, Nathan really took it upon himself to research some more companies until he came across one that truly caught his eye. It's not actually an adoption agency, per se, but rather, it's a marketing firm that helps you make an adoption profile, which they will send out to potential birth mothers across the United

States. The only drawback was that we had to have $16,000 up front with no guarantees of a successful adoption, although they did have a successful adoption rate within two years of 98 percent. If we went this route, this would be our last chance, as it would take up much of our finances—some of which we had already lost trying the international agency.

Nathan and I prayed over this new agency, something we didn't do much of with the first one, and we met with them via a phone conference. We both felt total peace over this and took that leap of faith, sending in the $16,000.

This is significant because money has never come easy to me. I have had to work, and work extremely hard, for all that I have. I have never been one where things were just handed to me, so to write out a check for $16,000 without a guarantee is something that took a lot of faith for me to do. The paperwork for this agency seemed effortless compared to the other agency, and this agency also constantly emailed and checked in with us.

While in the boat, there were some lessons that God had to show us and teach us. Two of these were patience and finding contentment in the waiting. These are two very hard things to do, especially when the enemy is always right there whispering words of doubt into your mind. The process took us a total of four, almost five, years from the first miscarriage until the adoption was finalized. That left a lot of time for doubts and frustrations. Habakkuk 3:17–18 states, "Though the fig tree does not bud and there are no grapes on the vines, though the olive crop fails and the fields produce no food, though there are no sheep in the pen and no cattle in the stalls, yet I will rejoice in the Lord, I will be joyful in God my Savior."

Nathan and I knew that we had to praise God no matter what. He deserved our praise when there were no sheep in the pasture, so to speak, and at every level of this process. It's really hard at the time to see how God is working, but looking back, my vision became clearer, even down to the people hired to help us along the way. They were each a blessing from God and strategically placed by Him.

In the meantime, Nathan and I began to bloom where we were planted. We decided that we would try to enjoy the process as much as we possibly could and realized that any day, we could be called and become instant parents, no longer being just the two of us. So we decided to enjoy the remaining time we had left of just being us. On top of this, Nathan became more active in our church, and I became more active with our military personnel. During the summer of 2017, my oldest nephew joined the Marine Corps. He was shipped to Parris Island in June. The Marine Corps boot camp is different than all the other boot camps in that the only line of communication they can have for twelve weeks are letters from home.

They are not allowed weekend phone calls or any other type of communication back home, so I began writing him letters weekly. On top of that, I began to write other trainees weekly that I found were not receiving any types of letters from back home—either they had no family or for some other reason. One of my godly gifts is encouragement, and I always thought it was such a small gift. However, it was huge in this ministry. I found writing and encouraging these Marines in training was easy to do, and I enjoyed doing it. I even found ways of incorporating scripture into their letters in the hopes that if they didn't know Christ already, they would seek Him out. At one point, I was writing up to four letters a week. Although I never received a reply back from any of them, other than my nephew and his one friend, I found it didn't matter. I knew this was what God wanted me to do in this time. This was the way I was to bloom. If I had had a child at this time, I may not have had the time to write. I had hoped that God would use my words, actually His words, of encouragement to give others the courage to take steps of faith. I heard a quote once saying broken crayons still color. I am not sure where the quote came from, but I do know that there have been some books and bible studies surrounding this quote. I decided I could still color no matter how broken I felt.

I also began reading a life-changing and life-challenging book called *Chase the Lion* by Mark Batterson. In the first few pages of the book, Mark lists a Lion Chaser's manifesto. In it, he states that we should set God-sized goals. Pursue God-given passions. Go after a dream that is destined to fail without divine intervention. Fight for your dreams, and if they don't scare you, well then, they are too small.

He states we should grab opportunity by the mane and don't let go! Live for the applause of nail-scarred hands. This book challenged my way of thinking from just being comfortable and arriving safely at each destination to really going for something that can only happen if God intervenes and wills it to be. I wrote down three things in my journal that I wanted to accomplish, each of which could only happen with God's intercession, two of which were writing this book and adopting a child.

In Mark's book, he talks about how many people hit a dead-end in their dream journey because they're waiting on God to go first, but really faith is taking the first step and then allowing God to reveal the second. He reminded me that sometimes, I have to stop praying and start praising God as if it has already happened. That is faith. Page 87 of Mark's book goes on to say that we need to take the first step toward our goals and even referenced the old 1989 Kevin Costner film, *Field of Dreams,* and the famous saying, "If you build it, they will come."

I know it sounds strange, but I began to hear God say to me that if I would build the nursery, He would fill it. I told Nathan what I heard God say to me, and being the amazing supporter he is, he said, "Okay! Let's do it," and so we did. We painted the walls and got new carpeting put down—everything we needed to do in order to get the room ready to be filled.

Now, God has a sense of humor. The moment we got the bedroom ready to go, I received a phone call from my cousin stating that he and his wife were going through a divorce, and he needed a place to stay until they could sell their house and he could get back on his own two feet. Well, God did fill the room. He just didn't fill it the way we thought He would.

This was around December of 2017. Of course, we knew that this is what God would want us to do, and we said yes to my cousin without batting an eye. Here again, we had to place our faith in Jesus. God's timing became even more of an importance to us because if we received a phone call now that we had a waiting child or birth mother, we would have to really move some stuff around. Our second spare room was where my home office was held, and that would need to be moved to our downstairs laundry room—not impossible, but definitely a project. Also, we would have to have our home study amended since we had another resident in the house.

This would cost us more financially, and also, it put us at risk of now being turned down. We just pressed on in faith, struggling to see God's perfect timing. We went from praying that any day we would get a phone call, to now praying that we wouldn't receive one for fear of being turned down and losing another chance at having a family. Trusting God during this time really tested us.

As God's perfect timing is always, well, perfect, my cousin sold his house pretty quickly and was able to find a new place to rent, all within about a three-month time span. He moved out in March of 2018, and a few weeks later on March 29, we received a phone call from our adoption agency stating we had been chosen for a baby girl due in July. Like I said, we didn't find God's humor amusing at the time, but looking back, all we could do was smile and shake our heads at ourselves and how small our faith was. It is really an awe-inspiring moment when God both shows up and shows off. God rewards obedience and faith. I don't know why I continue to do as the Israelites did and circle the mountain of disbelief. Hopefully, it won't take me forty years to stop doing this.

During the waiting period in the boat, I also found comfort in Hannah's story. In the book of 1 Samuel chapters 1 and 2, we learn about Hannah, a wife of a Zuphite man named Elkanah. He had two wives, one of which had and was able to bare children, both sons and daughters. The other was Hannah, who had no children and was unable to become pregnant. We learn in these chapters that the Lord had closed Hannah's womb, but Elkanah loved her even still. However, she continued to be in misery and anguish and deep grief, especially since her rival, who I am assuming to be Elkanah's other wife, would provoke her in efforts to irritate her.

One day, Hannah prayed to the Lord, asking Him to remember her, and if He gave her a son, she would give him to the Lord for all the days of his life. The scriptures state she was deeply troubled by her situation, and she poured her soul out to the Lord. The Lord remembered her, and in time, blessed her with a son of her own, Samuel.

Hannah made good on her promise, and as soon as the baby was weaned, she gave him to the Lord. This was Hannah's prayer then:

> My heart rejoices in the Lord;
> in the Lord my horn (strength) is lifted high.
> My mouth boasts over my enemies,
> for I delight in your deliverance.
> There is no one holy like the Lord;
> there is no one besides you;
> there is no Rock like our God.
> Do not keep talking so proudly
> or let your mouth speak such arrogance,
> for the Lord is a God who knows,
> and by him deeds are weighed.
> The bows of the warriors are broken,
> but those who stumbled are armed with strength.
> Those who were full hire themselves out for food,
> but those who were hungry are hungry no more.
> She who was barren has borne seven children,
> but she who has had many sons pines away.
> The Lord brings death and makes alive;
> he brings down to the grave and raises up.
> The Lord sends poverty and wealth;
> he humbles and he exalts.
> He raises the poor from the dust
> and lifts the needy from the ash heap;
> he seats them with princes
> and has them inherit a throne of honor.
> For the foundations of the earth are the Lord's;
> on them he has set the world.

He will guard the feet of his faithful servants,
but the wicked will be silenced in the place
of darkness.
It is not by strength that one prevails;
those who oppose the Lord will be broken.
The Most High will thunder from heaven;
the Lord will judge the ends of the earth.
He will give strength to his king
and exalt the horn of his anointed.

I love this prayer and have indeed prayed it myself to the Lord. I love that Hannah could now boast over her enemies, yet she remained humble, knowing that it was God who allowed her to prevail. She gave God all the glory, which is something Nathan and I strive to do in our own lives.

In this time of waiting, I found comfort in Hannah's story. I could empathize with her anguish and sorrow and deep grief. There are no words to describe the heartache that comes from learning your pregnancy is no more and that you will never see your baby on this side of eternity. The fact is, it's a loss, but the world doesn't see it that way. As a matter of fact, in the medical field, they don't even call the baby a baby, but rather a fetus. It's so hurtful when people say to you, "Oh well. You were only 'X' number of weeks along. Just try again." Sometimes, I felt like screaming, "I just lost my baby, and I am in mourning! How could you possibly be so inconsiderate to say that the answer is to just try again and forget what happened or act as if what happened didn't matter!" I know that people who didn't go through it just didn't understand, but some of the things they would say would cut right through me. As a matter of fact, I am sure I would have been saying the exact same things had I not gone through a miscarriage myself.

Then, there were the holidays. The silence of Christmas morning was the loudest noise we could hear. Mother's Day was horrendous. I found I even stopped going to church on Mother's Day Sundays because it was just too hard to see all of the other mothers that got to be honored, and here I was with two lost babies and wasn't able to stand to be counted in with the others. Instead, I had to remain seated in the pew, feeling like an utter failure for not being able to do the natural thing women were to do and give my husband a child of his own. The remembrance of our children and the pain of their losses were at an all time high on this day, not to mention the sideways glances and the looks of sadness and pity that I could see coming from those around me.

I also stopped going in to visit my mother and mother-in-law during this day. It was just too hard. Once, in May of 2017, Nathan received a text from one of his cousins that said, "Happy Mother's Day." A few seconds later, he received another text stating, "Oops. LOL. That text was supposed to go to your sister." We just looked at each other in utter shock. We knew it was a total accident, but I was hurting so badly inside, and she was just able to laugh it off without a second thought. I remember thanking God for allowing Nathan and I to go through the miscarriages. It made us better, more compassionate people. *How many times have I done that in the past to someone and just laughed it off without a second thought, totally ignorant of their feelings?* I hope and pray that I never do again.

What was even worse was when Father's Day rolled around, Nathan seemed to hardly be affected. I know that men are different than women in so many ways, but this made me feel like a failure too. *Why was he able to deal with this and I wasn't?* This started my battle with grieving in silence, which isn't healthy, but I felt as if I was being dramatic or reverting back to my mental health days of being extremely anxious and depressed.

In Hannah's story, it is also written how she was provoked by her rival, and I have to say that this happened to me, although maybe a little more subtle. In fact, I am not sure others even know they do it, but when you reach a certain age range, and you don't have children of your own, you begin to be ostracized from those in your friendship circles that do have children. I remember many times, sitting there with other women, wives of my husband's friends, having absolutely nothing to contribute to the conversations they were having and feeling so out of place.

They would go on and on about their children and the activities they were involved in or the new milestones taking place, and since no one really cared about my stories regarding my Jack Russell Terriers, I just sat there and listened, grieving internally, and putting on a fake smile acting as if I wasn't internally shutting down. On the flip side of this, now that we have been blessed with a child, we have been invited to events and social circles that wouldn't even have given us a second glance before.

I also started looking at other women who had babies that I didn't think was deserving of motherhood and let it resonate resentment and anger in myself. God had to scold me over this, reminding me that His ways are higher than mine. Isaiah 55: 8–9 states, "For my thoughts are not your thoughts, neither are your ways my ways, declares the Lord. As the heavens are higher than the earth, so are my ways higher than your ways and my thoughts than your thoughts." Again, I had to go back to the basics of who God is and stop placing myself higher than He. What right did I have to judge whom God allowed the blessing of children?

I am so glad that God has put Hannah's story into His gospel. What a comfort it was knowing that this happened in biblical times and that my feelings were normal, even if the world said they weren't. My friend had bought me a book named *Hannah's Hope*. It was written by Jennifer Saake, and in it, I really got an in-depth look into Hannah's story and was given the opportunity to see Jennifer's, as well as others' struggles. It was very uplifting to my spirit to know that others felt the same way and had the same thoughts and that I wasn't alone. The thoughts that would go through my head would sometimes make me feel so alone, but knowing others had the exact same state of mind brought me much comfort.

I later shared this book with my best friend who had suffered a stillborn birth and was struggling deeply with the tragic loss. She thanked me so many times for forwarding it on to her. She said that she couldn't put it down and found it to be of great encouragement.

Hannah's story later goes on to say that the Lord was gracious to her and blessed her with three more sons and two daughters. I cannot say for sure how many children God will bless us with, but we will take whatever the Lord gives us and shout praises to His name, and for the one He did bless us with, we had her dedicated to the Lord one Wednesday in the fall of 2018.

While sailing in the boat, we decided to start praying to God that we would praise Him and accept whatever was on the other side of the crossing. That's not to say that we wouldn't be disappointed if God's answer to our growing family was "no," but we would accept it and praise His name anyway. We faced the reality that God knew us better than we knew ourselves. His word says that before we were born, He knew us in the womb (Jer. 1:5), and He knows the number of hairs on our heads (Luke 12:7). God knew if we would make good parents and whether we would be able to handle the process and the challenges of parenting, so ultimately, we did want God's plan for us. Plus, we knew that what He had planned was bigger and better than anything we could even imagine. Maybe He even wanted us to be barren here on earth so that we would be free to spend our time in missionary work. Whatever the reason, we wanted God to know that we loved Him no matter. These weren't just words we spoke. We believed them and lived by them. We wanted to be all in with Jesus, no matter what that looked like.

The passage of Mark 4:36 states that there were other boats with them. I have to say that I have skipped over this part of the passage every time until one day when the Holy Spirit brought it to my attention. I cannot believe I passed over this and missed its significance. There were other boats with them, meaning there were others just like us and going through the exact same things. We were not alone in this journey. Others were taking this exact same voyage with the Lord. Once we started to make our adoption journey known, people came out in drones to tell us their stories. There were people who had successfully adopted or others who had friends or family members who had adopted children, and they wanted to share this with us. There were also those who had suffered miscarriages and infertility issues and could send us their empathy.

Once, during a Sunday night prayer service that our church holds every other Sunday, one couple came up to us and said that they have successfully adopted a baby girl from Honduras. It was twenty-eight years ago, but they wanted to give us hope and encourage us. They said that they had been visiting their child in Honduras for a couple of weeks as most countries participating in international adoptions have specific guidelines warranting the adopting parents to stay in their country for a certain amount of time before an adoption can be finalized. During the weeks they were down there, the two governments started changing their adoption laws, possibly taking the United States out of the equation of being able to adopt from Honduras. So, the couple was told to go back home to the United States without their child and let the attorneys take over.

The woman told me she went back home but could not stand knowing her child was in another country and that there was a chance she may not be able to ever go get her and bring her home, so without the blessing of the attorneys, she flew back to Honduras to fight for her daughter and for the adoption to be finalized. Her husband had to stay back home due to work purposes. It took her three weeks of fighting and working her way up the Honduras governmental ladder, but she never gave up her faith, asked for prayers from back home, and conquered the barriers with the shield of the Lord her God. This story left me in tears. God is remarkable in the way He can shove down barriers and work through any border, and what an example of God's strength in this woman.

Another woman from our church stated that she could empathize with us in the miscarriage department. She said that she and her husband had suffered multiple miscarriages, and although they would like to adopt, they have never had the finances come through for them in order to be able to take that step. Once, she said that she even found out that one of her pregnancies was a tubal pregnancy, and so even though the baby had a heartbeat, they had to remove it from her tube. She went on to say how incredibly deflating it was to finally have a viable pregnancy and have to make that decision to have it removed. She eventually had to have her uterus removed as well, removing all hope of having their own children.

I could go on and on with the incredible stories of men and women who have shared their testimonies with us and battled infertility with both successes and failures. Sadly, it took going through a miscarriage myself in order to grasp the significance and the hardship of it. I once acted as so many others. I was even so confident, arrogant actually, that this would never happen to me. I can truly say that even though I want my two children here with me on earth, I also would not want to go back to the person that I was before the miscarriages happened. God has allowed me to *see,* and now I can empathize with the others that are in this same boat and encourage them along the way. The scope of the people I can encourage, which is my spirit gift from God, just got vaster. Isn't it awesome how God can use something so tragic for good and for His purposes?

We remained in the boat for almost four years, and I got pretty sick of having sea legs. I was ready to dock this boat and move on to the next phase of my life—whether it was with or without children. Looking back, I wish I would have found my rejoice voice more often. Thankfully, God is faithful even when we aren't. He had our course charted, and we just had to hold on and have bigger faith.

CHAPTER 4

The Storms

A furious squall came up, and the waves broke
over the boat, so that it was nearly swamped.
Jesus was in the stern, sleeping on a cushion.
The disciples woke him and said to him,
"Teacher, don't you care if we drown?"
—Mark 4:37–38

Just as His word predicts, storms came our way. One storm we faced multiple times was from failed adoption opportunities.

One evening in the fall of 2016, our pastor called us up and explained that someone in our congregation (I will call her Mary for privacy purposes), reached out to him to inquire whether he knew of anyone that was looking to adopt a child. Of course, he knew we were trying, so he took the information for us and gave us a call. As it turned out, Nathan had been part of a discipleship Bible study with Mary, so Nathan knew her pretty well.

When we called her, she explained that her nephew had two boys, both under the age of four, and they were taken by the local CYS (Children and Youth Services) agency. Their father had overdosed on drugs and had been arrested. Mary was thrilled to know that we were interested in the possibility of adopting her great-nephews. Since we go to the same church, and since she was unable to adopt them herself, she felt this was and would be an amazing way to stay in their lives. This was not their father's first offense in this area, and we were told that CYS had been in and out of their home multiple times over this same issue, so they were looking to find a new, forever home for these two boys. Nathan took down all the information, and I called CYS the very next day. I had a really good feeling about this and allowed my thoughts to get swept up in the "what ifs." It seemed like God's fate and His way of intricately placing people to work together for His good. I barely slept that night due to the excitement and anticipation of calling CYS. That excitement was soon squashed and was very short-lived.

The agent at CYS that I had spoken with explained to me that I had actually been misinformed. They were still trying to place these boys back with their father and keep them united with their birth parents. I asked if they would be willing to keep Nathan and I's name on their file in case they ever came up for adoption and was told that our names and our information would be passed on to the case-worker but not to expect any type of call back from anyone. I was floored by that response. Why shouldn't I expect a phone call back? Why would the caseworker brush us off as potential parents for these two children?

I began to love these two boys that I had never met. I guess that is what is known as a mother's heart because my heart just burst at the seams with love that I wanted to pour over these two children. Nate and I fantasized about what Christmas would be like and started to think of things we could buy them and ways to decorate their bed-rooms. We thought that maybe neither one of them had ever owned a bicycle and that maybe something we could think of getting them. We thought about picking out a live tree with them and the noise and joy they would bring to our home on Christmas morning and every morning. I was heartbroken for these children, and I could not believe the way this CYS agent handled our phone call in an almost dismissive manner.

I remember thinking that CYS should be the hope for these children and should be manning the front lines for them, but it seemed to me as if the care of the children wasn't even being thought about, but rather the birth parents were the ones being catered to.

Here was a perfect opportunity for these two children to have a better, more stable home, and we were dismissed and swatted away like a fly on a dinner plate. At times during the phone conversation, it was even portrayed that I would be unworthy of adopting these boys, and I was silly for even asking. By no means am I judging Children and Youth Services or the agents and caseworkers working there. I cannot even begin to imagine what they go through and what they see daily; however, on the same spectrum, I was set aghast by how "the system" handled these cases.

I just remember finding this whole situation extremely eye-opening and all-around discouraging. Tears left my eyes often when I thought of these two boys and the situation that we couldn't help them get out of. Our hands were tied. While the system remained still on the issue, we also had to remain still. Believe me when I say that I believe that the children would do better in an environment where they got to stay with their natural parents. However, as I stated earlier, this was not this man's first offense, nor was there any type of proof that he was trying to change and better the situation for all of them.

We called Mary back and explained this all to her. We asked her to please keep us informed if their situation changes and these two boys do go up for adoption. She said she would and thanked us from the bottom of her heart for at least attempting.

I decided to call our local CYS agency back to ask if they would keep Nathan and I's name on file in case any children under the age of two came their way that needed a forever home. Once again, we were scolded by the agency. I was told that it is very rare that a child under the age of two comes through CYS needing adopted, and even when they do, they are what "everyone" wants, so we, once again, shouldn't expect a phone call. To say my jaw hit the floor was an understatement. She made us feel ashamed that we didn't want to adopt older children. Nathan and I have reasons for wanting our first adoption and first living child to be younger, but that agent didn't even care to ask us our reasoning or to even think that maybe we had a legitimate reason. We were automatically stereotyped as "one of those people." I was and am extremely disappointed in the way the county handles these situations. Again, only God knows their hearts and the things they have seen and continue to see daily, but I remember thinking how sorry it is for these children if this is their line of hope and defense.

As the disciples did in the above scripture, we couldn't help but question God in our hearts. We kept thinking, *Why wouldn't God allow these two boys to come into our home and allow them to get out of that situation?* We knew God cared about those two children more than we can even begin to understand, but it didn't make sense to us in any human way. Just as easily as those thoughts came, God had an answer for us. Isaiah 55:9 tells us, "As the heavens are higher than the earth, so are my ways higher than your ways and my thoughts than your thoughts."

Another six months passed, and we still hadn't gotten any hits from our adoption profile. There were a few cases that our home study caseworker had sent over to us and we tried for, but none of those ever opened up for us as actual opportunities. When she would send them over, she would also send the pictures. We would pray over the child and respond back if we felt the Lord's leading. It's funny how just seeing a picture of a child can bring your parenting imagination to life. Once I saw the picture, I could start picturing hugging them and holding their hands as we walked down the street. I could imagine them sitting across the dining room table from us and the conversations we would have. That is actually not a practice I would recommend as it made the heartbreak of a failed opportunity even greater.

One evening in the spring of 2018, Nathan received another phone call from Mary who said that, once again, her nephew had been arrested for drug abuse, and the two boys were having a hearing in two weeks to officially be placed in a need of adoption status.

I dreaded the phone call that I needed to make to CYS again, but I picked up the phone and asked them for the status. They stated that once again, we had been misinformed. They were having a hearing, but it was actually an evaluation for the parents. Immediately, I thought, *Imagine that!*

They were giving the parents one more chance to get straight and get these boys into a safe living environment. The agent said that it would probably be something like six months, and then they would check back in with the parents to make sure they were progressing through the program. Now, I was really getting upset with CYS. These two boys could have been out of this situation months ago and working on healing and adapting to a new, healthier environment, but instead, the justice system was going to leave them in that same, harmful environment. Coinciding were the thoughts of just how incredibly in-depth and intricate our home study had to be in order to even try to adopt a child and how that didn't seem balanced at all with what they allow birth parents to get away with. It didn't make sense to me that we had every inch of our lives and our home investigated, but it was perfectly fine to leave these children in such a toxic environment.

Again, I had to call Mary back with the sad news, and again, she thanked us for trying. A few months later, we heard from our pastor that Mary's nephew (these two boys' father), had been shot and killed. We attended the viewing to give her our condolences, and we did get to see a glimpse of the two boys. We watched them as they interacted with their birth mother who apparently struggled with the same issues. Seeing the boys in person gave us the closure we needed in this situation, however weird that may sound. We knew that God was not opening this door for us, and we needed to move on.

Mary gave us a picture of one of the boys to keep and pray over, which we do from time to time. Mary's nephew was a kindhearted individual that just couldn't win the battle over his addiction with drugs. That was the last we heard regarding those two boys, and even though I thought we could give these two an amazing life, this was not the door, nor the adoption, God had in mind for us.

Another storm we faced was dealing with the news of Nathan's sister's pregnancy. About a month or two after Nathan and I found out about our first miscarriage, we noticed the family seemed to be walking on eggshells around us and dodging certain questions.

One night, I told Nathan that I had a feeling his sister was pregnant and that everyone was probably afraid to tell us or just didn't know how to do so. Well, that was the exact case. One day, we were driving home from a Sunday visit with our family, and Nathan received a phone call from his sister giving him the news. If any of you reading this have gone through a miscarriage, you know the war of emotions my body immediately went through. My emotions waged war against each other internally.

First, I was excited for them. They had finally conceived after months of trying, and Nath and I were going to be an aunt and uncle again. However, there was also a large pit of despair and envy and jealousy and sadness, raging in my lower gut, and I hated that feeling. I knew it was wrong to feel that way, and I tried everything I could to make sure it never surfaced, but it was extremely hard to choose happiness for them. It was honestly a daily struggle for a long time, and it was something I had to cope with quite often. Although his family tried to shield us from it, there was no way of being able to shield us from it all, especially whenever a baby shower was being planned and when we could see the baby bump growing.

I hated how selfish and self-centered I was being, and I tried to control it and pray over it as much as possible, but the fact of the matter was that I was still grieving and in mourning over our loss. My stomach would wrench and churn whenever we would see how excited Nate's gram and great-aunt would get over the pregnancy. They began buying a ton of stuff for them, and it was incredibly deflating to be around. I just couldn't help but think about how our baby wouldn't get to experience this. On the day of her baby shower, Nathan and I actually had a wedding to attend. We had already RSVP'd that we would attend long before we knew the date of the shower, and I felt total relief that I had somewhere else to go besides sitting in that hall, watching everyone celebrate the upcoming birth of a new baby. But I also felt tremendous guilt. Why did I feel this way? Why couldn't I get over my own selfish feelings and let go, move on? I hated the emotions but didn't know how to fight against them.

In November of 2015, our nephew was born. As I woke up that morning to get ready for work, I had this strange feeling that today was going to be the day. I believe this was God's way of preparing me for the difficulty that this news was going to bring. Again, I dealt with a mixture of emotions, but this time, I was at least comforted by the fact that Nathan was feeling them too.

I think we felt every human emotion possible. We were happy and thrilled for our newest family member and for our sister and brother-in-law. However, we missed Gummy, and we were sad for our loss. We were sad that we would never hold our Gummy this side of heaven or even know whether Gummy was a boy or a girl. We sat in our family room downstairs that evening and just cried in each others' arms. We didn't have the courage or the emotional stability that night to go and do any type of visiting at the hospital, so we went the next morning after church. We went before actual visiting hours started so that we wouldn't be surrounded by a gathering of other family members in case we broke down. Even though I was crying inside, I put on a strong, happy front, and did what I knew the Lord would want me to do. *Will I ever be normal around children again? Will this resentment and anger and sadness last forever?*

> Journal Entry: November 9, 2015
> Our nephew was born over the weekend. He is really sweet, but it was really hard knowing that we would never get to see or hold our Gummy this side of heaven.
> Nate's sister said to us, "He needs a cousin." Her heart was truly in the right place, but that comment sliced through my heart like a hot blade. I caught my breath and held it so that I wouldn't cry. I wanted him to have a cousin too, and it pained me that I couldn't give him that or give Nathan a child of his own. God, help me to see the encouragement in her comment and not feel the sting of my failures!

We love our nephew so much, but the next few months continued to be a struggle, at least for me. Nathan seemed to be okay with everything now, and that, again, put me into a frenzy of inner madness. I began thinking that I just needed to get over it already and that something was seriously wrong with me for continuing to feel this way, but certain times, certain things just snuck into my thoughts and got me down.

One thing that was hard to deal with was that Nathan's grandmother never got to see us have a baby before she died, and it was hard to see her with her great-grandson.

Another storm we faced was with the constant barrage of questions of people wanting update statuses, as well as advice that others felt they should give out to us although we never asked for it. When Nathan and I decided to spread the news about pursuing adoption, we were met with the challenge of telling only those people who we thought would be supportive and pray for us. Throughout this entire journey, we have met so many people whose hearts have seemed to be in the right place, but truly I tell you, their words and actions have done us more harm than good. I believe it's in our human nature to think we have to say something or that we must have the answers and fix the situation. However, what Nathan and I have found to be the most helpful has been in the ones who will pray for us or just offer us a hug and a smile or even just lend us an ear, rather than those who felt they had to have an answer for us.

People have told us that we were young and to just keep trying. They would proceed to tell us of others they knew who suffered miscarriages and what the answers were for them. We also had those that had opinions on adoptions, whether good or bad, they didn't seem to care, but wanted to make sure we knew their thoughts on the matter.

One time at church, I had a woman approach me and introduce herself and her husband. She asked me if I had any children, and I didn't want to go into the entire ordeal, so I told her that we didn't, to which she replied, "Oh, are you one of those career women?" I cannot even remember my response to her; maybe I just blinked. I'm not really sure, but I know it stung and showed me just how much anger and bitterness I had been hanging onto.

During the adoption process, all the paperwork and background checks and home studies did not surmount to the toughness of the waiting—didn't even come close. Every single day, Nathan and I would wake up and think, *Today might possibly be the day we* get *"the call."* But then evening would come and then night with no phone call, telling us we have a little bundle waiting to call us mom and dad, or a birth mom who was impressed by our adoption profile and decided we would be the exact parents she would want to adopt her child.

What made the waiting even worse were the constant questions from people who knew we were going through the process and who wanted to be updated constantly on the status. We knew in our hearts that they were just as excited as we were, but the enemy used that to slowly creep into our thoughts. Nathan and I are truly peaceful and content people, and we have said throughout this entire process that we want God's will in our lives no matter what that means, and we will deal with the consequences if that does mean no children for us at all. But whenever people are constantly coming up to us and asking us if we have heard anything yet, and when we say no, seeing the disappointment in their faces, we can feel the enemy creep in and start to steal our peace. We start wondering what is wrong with our profile that no one has chosen us so far. We also start to feel our patience leaving and stop waiting on God's timing and start thinking it should be happening in our time. So, we have had to really think about whom we tell about the process, so that we choose the ones that will truly pray for us and who will not constantly barricade us for updates.

Once, we even thought about changing our adoption profile, thinking that maybe we emphasized Jesus and our faith too much and that this was possibly what was turning people away from choosing us. However, we quickly squashed that. We picked up right away that that was the enemy, trying to steal and remove Jesus from our lives. We believed that it would be because of Jesus that we would be able to adopt and vowed we wouldn't remove it from our profile no matter what. We also would rather never be chosen than to remove the name of Jesus from our lives, our search, and our hearts. We were not ashamed of the name of Jesus and wanted to prove that to Him now and in this way. Later, it would be made known that our birth mother chose us because of our faith and love for Jesus.

We have also had people offer "advice." I put those in quotes because even though Nathan and I know that mostly these peoples' hearts were in the right place, at times, their words have felt like daggers in our backs and have really knocked us down. For example, after our second miscarriage, we had someone tell us that the third time is a charm. I know that it was meant to be encouraging, however, it made me feel as if our first two children and their deaths didn't matter and that I should just brush that under the rug.

I had one lady come up to me and say that the reason that God hasn't blessed me with children is because I am a bad and sinful person. She told me to just read the Old Testament, and I will see it's filled with stories of how God used infertility to punish His people. If anyone is reading this that has had the same thing said to them, I want to share with you what God has said to me about that. It is true that God used this as a tool in the Old Testament, before Jesus's coming, but He said that He sent His Son, Jesus Christ, to die for us, and with that, our sins have been buried, so if anyone ever says that to you again, look to the cross. John 9:3 states, "Neither this man nor his parents sinned," said Jesus, "but this happened so that the works of God might be displayed in him."

We have also had people say to us that they know how we feel. On one particular occasion, a gentleman was talking to Nath and me one day and said that he knew exactly how we feel and went through the exact same thing. He continued to tell us how he had accompanied his wife to her first prenatal visit (the one where you get to hear the heartbeat for the first time that we have never gotten to experience). He said at first that they couldn't find the baby's heartbeat, so he and his wife became extremely scared and started thinking the worst-case scenarios, but then, they found the heartbeat, and what a relief it was. They went on to have a normal pregnancy with their baby being born healthy. We don't deny the stress of this situation for them, but ultimately, he and his wife got to hold their child and raise their child. We have not. They ultimately heard the heartbeat. We never did.

Some say to us that if we want to have a child of our own, to adopt, and it will happen. We have heard this a countless number of times of where somebody knows somebody who had trouble conceiving on their own, so they decided to adopt, and wouldn't you know it, they had a baby of their own. Once after telling our story at church, we had someone come up to us and say, "I know God is going to bless you with a child." Although we try to appreciate the encouragement, we know that unless God decided to speak to them at that very moment about our current situation and status, which maybe He did and maybe He didn't, but which we doubted, that that person had no idea whether we were going to be blessed with a child or not.

A few months after the miscarriage of Gummy, my best friend texted me to let me know she was pregnant. She said that she didn't know how to tell me because she didn't want to be inconsiderate of all the feelings and grievances I was going through, but she also didn't want me to find out through someone else. I appreciated that more than I will ever be able to express to her. Her compassion refreshed my soul, and I was over the moon for her and her husband. However, about six months later, we were reading the newspaper and found an obituary that took the wind right out of us. We had read that she had delivered a stillborn, preterm baby on Thanksgiving Day.

Not long after reading that obituary, she had texted me asking if I would come to the funeral. She said she understood if it was too much for me but that my being there would mean the world to her. Nathan and I knew that we would never miss being there for her and her family, so on a rainy Saturday morning, we made the journey to the graveside. It was the smallest casket I had ever seen in my entire life. I remember thinking how brave and strong my best friend truly was, and at that very moment, Nathan and I thanked God for taking Gummy when He did. We both knew that if we had miscarried any later, or at the time my best friend did, that we may not have been able to withstand the pain of it.

Our second miscarriage happened in the spring of 2017. I had started seeing a new primary care physician and had been talking to her about the increased frequency of migraines I had been having. She decided to order an MRI of my brain with contrast. Prior to the procedure, I was asked multiple times if there was any way that

I could be pregnant. I insisted that it wasn't possible, but a few days prior to the procedure, I realized I was two or three days late, so just to be certain, I took a pregnancy test. It was positive. I am ashamed to admit that I wasn't even excited about it. Both Nathan and I had the exact same emotion about it and decided to keep a level head until we got through the first and hard nine weeks before letting ourselves get any type of excitement stirred. I called my physician and cancelled the MRI procedure.

About four weeks later, in the middle of the night, I felt a sharp cramp that awakened me from sleep. I knew that at that very moment the Lord had taken our second baby to glory. I had the exact same sharp cramp during my first pregnancy, and it was also in the middle of the night. I now realized that was the moment the Lord had taken Gummy as well. Like I stated earlier, I had attributed it to possible gas pains, but now I knew better. A few weeks later, the bleeding started. This miscarriage did happen naturally, and I didn't have to get a D&C performed, but it was still full of feelings of despair.

At that point in time, Nathan and I decided to go back to using contraceptives. My body just felt beat up at the age of thirty-five, and I was tired of going through the pain mentally and physically. Nathan was feeling the mental drain of it all as well. He was amazing through everything. He went to every appointment with me and shared in the tears and fears and joys. God could not have given me a better companion through this.

It was after this second miscarriage as well that we started seeking medical advice to see if there was some sort of medical explanation for it all. We started in our hometown, but honestly, they just didn't seem to care enough or want to help us get some answers, so we looked into a world-renowned hospital in the city about an hour away from us.

There, I underwent a plethora of tests and exams. Once, while we were reading over the paperwork they had given us and seeing the multiple tests that they could possibly request, I looked over and noticed my husband's face looked a little ashen. Apparently, he read that they may ask to do a sperm count on him. His fears were squashed pretty early though because they said that they ruled out a problem with his sperm counts since we didn't seem to have a problem getting pregnant. We just had problems staying pregnant, so we knew it was an issue with my body. There was another blow to my self-worth.

So, I did undergo a series of tests to check my reproductive process. They wanted to rule out endometriosis specifically, which they were able to do. All of my hormonal and thyroid blood counts came back normal as well, so that was another avenue ruled out. The next avenue would be to do some genetic testing; however, they warned me that this usually does little good other than to give peace of mind. If it was a genetic reason, it wouldn't help me with the infertility issues but would only serve to explain them. I am not a big fan of hospital procedures, needles or blood, so going through testing is an extremely stressful thing for me to do. In the end, we decided not to undergo the genetics testing. We decided to let it remain as it was, a mystery.

After the first miscarriage and especially after the second, I started to hate, loathe even, being around other women who were mothers. I felt that they mocked me in some sort of way. They never had to speak a word, but I felt their hidden stares and pity; the way they would stop talking around me as if they were sparing me or didn't feel I had adequate conversation to add. Honestly, I had no idea whether this was even true, but it became true in my mind. I hated being around mothers, especially when they started complaining about their child's sleep schedule or whatever else they may have had going on. *Didn't these women appreciate what they had? Don't they realize that I would give anything to have these "problems?"* There were many times when David's plea was at the forefront, "My tears have been my food day and night, while people say to me all day long, 'Where is your God?'" (Ps. 42:3).

All these storms were hard to bear at times, each one its own wave, crashing into our boat and rocking it from side to side. Sometimes, it felt as if we would capsize or that all we were doing was taking in and swallowing water. Once we got through one wave, the next one was always right behind.

One thing that the Holy Spirit allowed me to note was the word, "nearly," in the passage above. They were *nearly* swamped but never completely. This held true in our journey as well. There were so many times when I felt the waves were going to cripple me to the point of drowning, but they never did. They always seemed to subside just in time, sometimes with a friendly, encouraging word or a much needed reprieve. Once, Nathan and I decided to get away and draw closer to God, so we rented a cabin in the Smokey Mountains of Tennessee. We took Christian books with us and just spent days reading God's word and praying. We put nothing else on our agenda other than this, and we drew so much strength from that time with God. I highly encourage anyone going through this, if possible, to get away and just be with God. We came back feeling so refreshed and ready to plunge back into the battlefield of infertility. I yearn daily for the peace I felt on this trip and in this time with my Father.

> Journal Entry: Monday, March 16, 2015
> Going to Tennessee in three days. Need this break from winter and the miscarriage. Want to use this time to draw into Christ and God's Word and maybe get some answers.

There were many days where Nathan and I faltered in our faith or wanted to give up and give in. We would allow ourselves to feel the emotions and sometimes wallow in self-pity, but then we would get back up, dust ourselves off, and keep on. We had told God and ourselves that we would be okay with whatever decision He had for us, and we needed to honor that. One thing we always tried to do was to put a smile on our faces and be positive throughout and find God's reasoning because we truly believed there was one. We just had to wait it out to find it out.

My life verses are that of Psalm 46:5, "God is within her, she will not fall," and verse 10, which states, "He says, 'Be still, and know that I am God.'" Sadly, God has had to continuously remind me of these two facts, none more so than going through this process. I am a person that suffers with self-worth, and I have strong tendencies to have to be in control of everything. Throughout these storms, it was hard to remain confident and positive. It was also hard for me to think of myself as a worthy person. I dealt with feelings of failure, guilt, and very low self-esteem. I was a woman and should have been able to supply my husband with his own children, but I couldn't, and what was worse, I didn't know the reason why in order to be able to fix it.

God also had to remind me to pray and trust. I felt at times that this was all I was doing though and that the Lord wasn't listening. Habakkuk 1:2 says, "How long, Lord, must I call for help, but you do not listen?" This is what I felt was happening. I was sure God called us to adopt, but then, there were times when a long stretch of time elapsed without any news or forward progression. In fact, there were many times we either weren't making progress at all or were backtracking. Going back to the basics of who God is (loving, peaceful, all-knowing, just, and sovereign) helped me to deal with these periods of drought. Habakkuk 1:12 says, "Lord, are you not from everlasting?" Habakkuk 2:3 says, "Though it linger, wait for it; it will certainly come and will not delay." When God promises something, He will deliver it. He will also give us the strength to endure the wait and the weight of the storms.

CHAPTER 5

Is Jesus Asleep?

> Jesus was in the stern, sleeping on a cushion.
> The disciples woke him and said to him,
> "Teacher, don't you care if we drown?" He
> got up, rebuked the wind and said to the
> waves, "Quiet! Be still!" Then the wind
> died down and it was completely calm.
> He said to his disciples, "Why are you so
> afraid? Do you still have no faith?"
> —Mark 4:38–40

Nathan and I have such little faith at times, and we talk about how mad at ourselves we get over that fact. Multiple times throughout this, Jesus has had to ask us why we were so afraid, and why did we have such little faith.

Our pastor and his wife take vacations to Florida, and while they are on vacation, they will attend a certain church on Saturday nights. One particular Saturday night service they attended happened to be the church's Mother's Day service.

The pastor at the Floridian church had gone on to say that he knew of a family that had tried to conceive for years, and he was happy to announce that after all the prayers, God had finally blessed them with a baby. He wanted to share this Mother's Day with not only the women who had already had children but also with those who have not yet been blessed with children of their own. The pastor opened the service for anyone who was trying to conceive that had not yet, or if anyone knew of such persons, to come forward and stand in the gap for them. Our hometown pastor and his wife are absolutely amazing people. They went up there and stood in the gap for us. Jesus is not asleep on our situation.

One Wednesday afternoon in March of 2018, I had the day off of work and took an afternoon nap after working on house chores all morning. When I awoke, I had a missed phone call from our adoption agency with a voicemail. The voicemail stated that we had a woman interested in our profile and wanted to meet with us via phone call to talk about the potential of us adopting her unborn child. I called Nathan at work and caught him by surprise as well.

We called the agency back and were told that our birthmother lived in Utah and had been assaulted and was looking to place the baby up for adoption. She loved our profile and wanted to learn more about us, so we set up a date and time to call her (we will call her Amy to allow her privacy).

We hit it off with Amy right away. She shared our free spirit and love of sports. We even liked rival NFL teams, so Nate had a field day teasing her about that. We openly shared our adoption story with her and the reasons for which we were going through the process. She also openly shared her story. Amy told us that she had a friend that wanted to be more than that even though she clearly told him she didn't, and instead of him respecting that, he forced himself on her. She went on to say that she couldn't keep the baby and be able to heal and move on with her life. She is active military and already has a four-year-old son and just couldn't have this addition to her family.

She said that so many people told her to have an abortion, but as a Christian, she knew that option was not the right one and would go against her beliefs. She said family members also said they would adopt the baby to at least keep the baby in the family, but what they were failing to realize was the fact that it would still be a constant reminder to Amy of the trauma she had experienced.

Amy said she came across our adoption agency and decided to contact them. They gave her a wide variety of profiles, but she admitted that as soon as she read ours, she knew we were the ones. She said that she even had her friend look over all the profiles, and she picked us too.

Over the next few weeks, we continued to keep in contact with her via text messages and emails, and in the month of April, she officially asked us to be the adoptive parents. Words cannot express the joy we felt. Our agency told us to keep our hearts open but our feet on the ground because the baby wasn't due until July, and there was so much that could change, including Amy changing her mind, so we did just that, or at least we tried to.

We first told our pastor and his wife. The second was our best friends, and then we told the remainder of our family and friends. Everything with Amy became seamless. We kept in contact at least weekly. She would send us the ultrasound pictures and keep us informed of the baby's health and growth progression. Jesus was captaining the boat. We really had an amazing birth mother. Once, she had asked us if we wanted to send her over voice recordings for baby girl that she would put next to her belly so that the baby could get used to our voices. That was an amazing opportunity for us to get to be a part of.

The paperwork was another thing altogether and not seamless. It had been since 2016 since our original home study was done, so we had to redo a lot of the paperwork, clearances, and home walk through for the attorneys. By June's end, I was "over" adoption paperwork. Nate and I were ready to go get our baby girl.

We decided to drive the 1,900 miles versus fly. Neither Nate nor I really enjoy flying, and flying home with a newborn made us totally uneasy. Amy was set to be induced on July 16 or 17; however, the week before, she said she highly doubted baby girl was going to wait that long, so on a Tuesday, we set out for Utah. I had never been west of Ohio, so I was looking forward to the new scenery. We had the most beautiful drive out, and we made it before baby girl decided to come. Jesus was in control.

During the drive out, we received an email from the attorney's office asking us if we had discussed naming the child with Amy. We hadn't because we really weren't sure what that process was, so I texted Amy and asked her what she wanted to do. She said that she was good with us naming her. We let it up to her whether she would want to know the name, and she said that she would like that, so we told her what we were thinking. Nate loves the Chicago Cubs, so we found a way to name her after them. The middle name was a combination of Nate's late grandparents.

Amy texted back stating that we would not believe this, but when she had been thinking of a name for baby girl, she came up with the exact same middle name, and the middle name we both picked out was not a common one, and she also picked the name using a combination of her late parents' names. Talk about knowing Jesus is commanding this ship. What are the odds that we would pick the exact same middle name? Our minds were blown.

We owe Amy so much that we will never be able to repay her for. Not only does she serve our country as an active military member, but she has given us a hope of a family of our own. Plus, she chose life and not abortion.

Throughout this experience, God has given us an amazing glimpse of just how much He is in control. He has allowed us the ability to trace this plan for us all the way back to Nathan and I's teenage years.

As I stated before, Nathan and I were high school sweethearts. Nathan's grandfather passed away when Nathan was just 16. After his passing, Nathan's grandmother had to process all the paperwork that comes along with a passing family member. One phone call she made was to Black Lung where she got a sweet representative that kindly explained to her the benefits that she would be entitled to. This included collecting a monthly type of pension that her husband had, which she didn't even know existed. She ended up placing this monthly check into a savings plan—each month doing the same as the month before. Fast-forward to almost twenty years later to her passing. She had saved that money each month, never using any of it, and she left a portion of that in the will for Nathan that just so happened to be the answer to our financial adoption needs. How beautiful and intricate is our God? He allowed us to see that He was planning this adoption from when we were teenagers. He planned it down to even the representative that Nathan's grandmother had gotten on the phone at Black Lung. Perhaps, if she had gotten a different representative, they would have never told her the benefits she was entitled to, and the finances would not have been there. Jesus deserves our praise always. Is He sleeping at the helm? Maybe it seems like it, but He's still in complete control always. His ways truly being higher than anything I could even dream. At this time, I hoped and prayed that God would allow us an even further glimpse back into the adoption plan He had for us, and once again, God answered.

Journal Entry: June 4, 2016
Our adoption meeting is three days away. We need a miracle, and nothing short of, to find the finances. We really feel that we are hearing from God to adopt, so we are expecting that miracle and praising him in advance for already making this happen. We serve an amazing God, and although we still have doubts, we continue to pray for guidance.

Journal Entry: June 7, 2016
The adoption meeting wasn't successful. This company we looked into only accepts open adoption candidates, which Nate and I don't want to do. We will continue to look for other options, Lord willing.

Journal Entry: Monday, June 20, 2016
This past Saturday was Nate's grandmother's funeral. She is missed so much already. And how amazing is our God? We found out that she had willed approximately $20,000 to Nate, which will give us (or at least get us close) to what we need for the adoption. God is good!

Another example of God's control appeared to us a few weeks after we came back from Utah with our baby girl. We went to visit my paternal grandmother, which would be her great-grandmother. She told us that when she was a little girl, she had asked her parents for an African-American baby doll. All her other brothers and sisters made fun of her, but she had wanted this doll for some reason, and so, her parents got it for her. She said it was funny because the sisters that had previously made fun of her now only wanted to play with that baby doll as well. I didn't pick up on this at the time, but a few days later while rocking baby girl to sleep, I realized that God had showed me how He was preparing her great-grandmother's heart for her. How incredible. I just cried once it had hit me, as once again, I was totally in awe of how intricate and highly crafted our God is.

Jesus also made sure we had a Christian support group surrounding us at all times, especially since there were those who were unsupportive and making sure we knew it. He intricately placed friends and family, especially those of our church, in our lives to pray continually for us and even others who have gone through the same or similar situations that could really empathize with our struggles.

Once, we were invited to our friends' house for a house-warming party they were hosting in celebration of the recent purchase of their home. We were one of the last couples to leave. As we were walking to our vehicle, we noticed the car of a couple who had supposedly left about ten minutes before us. They were actually waiting for us to come out because they had something they wanted to speak to us about but wanted to do it in private. They had said that they had been praying for us and over our situation and wanted to offer us a surrogacy, meaning our good friend would carry our baby for us, if we would want to go this route.

Tears welled up in my eyes. This was one of the most selfless things I had ever encountered. We had known this couple since we were young. They also graduated high school with Nathan and I, so we have known them a very long time, and to think they would be willing to sacrifice this for us was incredible. I don't even have the words to pen here. It was awe-inspiring.

Nathan and I knew that this wasn't an alley we had wanted to take, nor the one God chose for us, but to know that there were people out there that wanted to help us in this way and give us this opportunity was extremely humbling and made us feel so loved.

When we were thinking Jesus was asleep, I believe it was because He was just laying back and watching us move in faith. Our relationship with Jesus had to work two ways, and we had to do our part too even though He knew the way that we would take (Job 23:10). This is a concept I forget a lot of the time. I am always praying and asking God to move and take the first steps, but many times, He is resting at the stern of the boat, waiting for me to move in faith and take initiative.

I believe that mediocrity is a Christian's enemy, and in order to be exceptional, we have to let God refine us. This happens through trials and storms. The beginning and end of my adoption journey were extremely important in my faith walk and also extremely rewarding, but the most important part of the trip was in the middle, during the storms. It was here that my faith began to grow bigger and stronger and here that I leaned on my Abba on a consistent basis. If we want to wear our gold crowns like the kings and queens we want to be, we have to let the gold of that crown be refined by our Lord. Going through these trials stunk, and I hated every minute of it, but looking back, it was the best part. It was here I learned how to be more compassionate and stronger and here that I became modeled more like my Savior.

It's even said that we are to be joyous in our trials and tribulations. "In all this you greatly rejoice, though now for a little while you may have had to suffer grief in all kinds of trials. These have come so that the proven genuineness of your faith-of greater worth than gold, which perishes even though refined by fire-may result in praise, glory and honor when Jesus Christ is revealed" (1 Peter 1:6–7). Again, we are told to find joy in trials in James 1: 2–4, "Consider it pure joy, my brothers and sisters, whenever you face trials of many kinds, because you know that the testing of your faith produces perseverance. Let perseverance finish its work so that you may be mature and complete, not lacking anything."

I love that these passages' note to remain joyous in *all kinds* of trials. No trial is singled out. God wants us to be joyous in any we face. This is something I have failed at continually, but I have not given up on trying to do better. Even while awaiting our news of a baby, I started finding joy in the waiting; by just enjoying my husband and I's time together without children and being able to just pick up and go whenever and wherever we felt like it, by enjoying having a full-time career, and by being able to just take a nap anytime of the day. Although, some days, it was really hard for me to be joyous in the stillness, I did try to find a way to praise God no matter what. I would even go through old journal entries to remind myself of His goodness and the many blessings He had lavished me with in the past.

Jesus was in control the entire time, and we would have been able to see this if we would have looked for it. We needed to keep our eyes open to the many blessings that were all around us. Jesus was surrounding us on all sides even if we thought He wasn't or thought He was asleep. The fact of the matter is God knows. He knows the depths of the sea trial in which He has asked you to travel. He knows the fears, anxieties, and ambitions that hide deep in your heart. His word tells us that He puts our tears in a bottle. (Ps. 56:8). There was never a time when He wasn't in total control of our journey, our checkbook, or our storms. When He has tried me, I shall come out as gold (Job 23:10).

CHAPTER 6

Squalling Waves

A furious squall came up, and the waves broke
over the boat, so that it was nearly swamped.
—Mark 4:37

We made the 1,900–mile journey to Utah in about two and a half days. I enjoyed the entire trip out. The differences in states and sceneries were breathtaking, and I got to experience first hand what others meant when they called the west God's Country and Big Sky. Driving through Wyoming, I felt as if I was in my own personal snow globe with blue skies and the whitest, puffiest clouds surrounding me on all sides. It was beautiful to look out of the passenger side window and see nothing but God's masterpiece in incredible rock formations and mountains and to look around 360 degrees and not see any type of building or manmade structure. I remember closing my eyes and thanking God for this experience and for His imagination and beauty.

We arrived in Utah around noon on a Thursday and texted Amy to let her know we made it and made plans to meet up for dinner that afternoon after her final doctor's appointment. Meeting our birth mother face-to-face for the first time was surreal. She was five feet and petite with a baby bump that stuck out so far, I wasn't sure how she was able to hold it up. It seemed to be completely out of proportion to her tiny figure. To see that baby bump just melted my heart. I kept telling myself to make sure I wasn't staring, but I just couldn't help it. It was hard to grasp the thought that Nate and I's baby girl was right there, and I wanted to see if she was moving in that belly.

We had a wonderful dinner. People have asked us what it was like, and we just tell them it was just as if we were meeting with an old friend. The conversation flowed easily. I feared it would feel awkward, yet it didn't. We really got to know a lot about Amy—about her family, her interests, and the type of mother she was to her then four-year-old son. We also told her a lot about us and our journey and what our lives were like back home. After dinner, she asked us if we would be willing to walk around the mall with her for a bit, and we jumped at the chance. Not only did we get to spend more time learning about our birth mother, but we also got the chance to try and get that baby moving. Getting to know Amy better was extremely important to us. We wanted to learn as much about her as we possibly could in order to be able to tell baby girl one day all about her.

Friday, we took a day to ourselves and went to see a few attractions near our hotel. We really wanted to sight see, but we were afraid to roam around too far just in case Amy would go into labor, so we went to see some museums and took to some local shopping. Saturday and Sunday were a lot like Thursday. Saturday, we took a day trip to Salt Lake City where Amy showed us around the city, which was of total interest to Nathan since it was the city that once held the winter Olympics. Sunday, Amy invited us to church with her, and I have to say, this was my favorite part. To stand in church next to Nathan and Amy with her baby bump sticking out and sing songs of praises to our Lord and Savior, Jesus Christ, was one of those "awe" moments, those "I cannot believe I am standing here right now" surreal moments. After church, we enjoyed an afternoon lunch together, after which, we said goodbye until we would meet again the next day—induction day. Amy promised to let us know the moment she heard from the hospital with the time of day we were all to be there on Monday, and making good on her promise, she texted us later that evening stating the hospital wanted her to be there at 8:00 a.m.

We hardly slept a wink that night, and later, Amy would tell us the same held true for her. We were on the road by 7:30 a.m., heading toward the hospital, when Amy texted us and said the hospital delayed her an hour and now wanted her to be there at 9:00 a.m. instead. So, having an extra hour to spare, Nate and I found an IHOP nearby and had some breakfast. I couldn't eat. My nerves were shot. The same held true for Nathan, although he was at least able to stomach eating a little bit of breakfast.

We pulled into the parking lot of the hospital at the same time as Amy. The feeling of walking in together with our birth mother was another one of those moments where you cannot put your feelings into words.

After about an hour of waiting and getting registered, they showed Amy to her room. They also gave Nate and I our own room, which was an incredibly nice gesture. We were relieved to hear they had done this wonderful thing for us and just knew God's hand had blessed us in this way. Even though Amy had sent us ultrasound pictures and pictures of the heartbeat over the past few months, we were never actually able to hear the beating noise itself. So when they placed the fetal heart monitor on her belly, and we heard the heartbeat for the first time, our hearts just about leapt out of our chests. Nathan and I looked right at each other, and we had the biggest grins on our faces, and at 4:06 p.m., approximately seven hours after the start of the induction, we heard the screaming cries of our baby girl. "Before I formed you in the womb I knew you, before you were born I set you apart" (Jer. 1:5).

Amy was incredible and allowed us both to remain in the delivery room, and the hospital staff also instructed us where to stand, so that when the baby came out, we would be able to see her and touch her right away. When they placed her into the bassinette right next to where we were standing, tears began immediately welling up in our eyes. We finally got to see the most beautiful creature we had ever seen in our lives. I cannot remember a time when I saw such little fingers and toes. She was perfect. Once they got her cleaned up, we were able to hold her, and the nurses and staff took photos for us. I remember yelling "thank you" so loud over to Amy after praising and thanking God for His gift to us. God is so faithful, and His promises are true. Almost three years prior was when He answered our adoption question, and we finally got to see all the hard work and patience come to fruition.

Once we took baby girl to our room, we took so many pictures and were texting everyone we could think of and got the most incredible responses. It was with great pleasure that we got to show our friends and family that God Almighty still answers prayers. The entire rest of that evening was spent just praising God and sitting in awe. There were absolutely no words. Isn't that just the way of our Lord? He can totally leave you in utter silence, stunned by His glory and works.

I cannot stop the text here and go on to the next chapter, telling you the remainder of the trip went seamlessly because that wasn't the case at all. The following day shook us to our core beings, stripping us down to raw faith, and causing us to call on our great prayer warriors back home.

When we first began speaking with Amy, back at the beginning of the process, she had said to us that she had wanted no contact with the baby and was contemplating having either a closed adoption, meaning no contact after the relinquishment of the baby, or possibly having a semi-open adoption, meaning some contact after relinquishment in the form of pictures and letters, but no visitations. However, that began to change. It was slow at first, but then, she really began wanting more and more contact with baby girl.

The day of the birth, Amy had called us and asked us if we wanted to have dinner with her, and we agreed to that. We asked her if she wanted us to bring baby girl up to her room with us or if she wanted us to place her in the nursery. She said to go ahead and bring her up and that she did want to hold her. That visit went extremely smooth, with tons of laughter, friendship, and encouragement.

We then took baby girl back to our room and enjoyed the remainder of the evening with her until we placed her in the nursery for the night. We wanted to keep her in our room but knew the nurses and staff would be checking on her every few hours, and we thought why not enjoy the last few nights of sleep we would be getting for quite some time.

The next morning, at 6:00 a.m., I woke Nathan up so that we could go get the baby. I couldn't wait to see her any longer, and as Nathan and Amy were the only ones with the wristbands that allowed access to get baby girl from the nursery, I had to wake my poor husband from his sleep. Later that morning, Amy contacted us again asking us if we wanted to have breakfast with her. We had already eaten but went down to keep her company while she had her breakfast. This was also when she informed us she would not be signing the relinquishment papers today. She had decided, along with the social worker, to give herself some more time—until eight thirty the next morning to be exact. We also learned from the pediatrician on call that he would hold the discharge until the next day as long as baby girl remained healthy.

We were adopting this child from the state of Utah, which allows the relinquishment papers to be signed no earlier than twenty-four hours after delivery, but we were hoping that Amy would sign them at the twenty-four-hour mark so that we could get the adoption paperwork started with the state of Utah and their ICPC (Interstate Compact on the Placement of Children) process. The ICPC process is an agreement held between all fifty states and allows for the legal transport of the adopted child from the state of the adoption to the home state. Without the relinquishment paperwork and without being discharged, our attorneys were not able to begin our ICPC paperwork, and so delaying our eventual 1,900–mile journey home.

Without signing the relinquishment paperwork, Amy still maintained all the parental rights to baby girl, so any tests run, and any decisions made regarding vaccinations, were ultimately decided upon by Amy. However, the hospital had no problems coming down to our room to get our insurance information to bill us for the said procedures and vaccinations. To us, this summed up the whole adoption process—no rights or guarantees but all the risks and financial responsibility. We didn't feel respected at all. Instead, we felt as if everyone only thought of us as the responsible financial party and not her adoptive parents.

Also, being eight states away from our home state, all medical bills were going to be processed as out of network, in which we have a $10,000 individual deductible, not including any copayments or coinsurances that may also be due, so by having us delay discharge by another day, put thoughts of financial doubt and frustration into our heads. Now, obviously, we wanted what was best for baby girl's health, but we were also allowing Satan a foothold in our thoughts in this manner. What's more, the social worker's estimated cost turned out to be lower compared to what would later be requested of us. (As an adoptive parent, you are responsible for any counseling and social services used by the birth mother. In some cases, you may even be responsible in helping a birth mother pay off some of her financial debts, medical bills, etc.).

On top of this, Amy changed her mind and decided to name baby girl after all. She knew that we would ultimately amend the birth certificate to give baby girl the name of our choosing, but she wanted the first name this baby would have to be in sequence with hers. This just floored us. Furthermore, Amy started requesting more and more time with the baby—each time we could see her getting more attached. We began to see a change in Amy's heart, and as a part-time mother, I could see her struggling more and more with the decision she was making.

Nathan and I believed, and still hold true to it, that Amy deserved all the compassion and respect that she was getting, and we cannot imagine the level of difficulty a decision of this magnitude must entail, but not one person, other than our lawyer, seemed to understand that we had a lot at stake in this process too. We also had a lot of emotions running wild with a lot at stake and much to lose. The weight of it all started to overpower me. I could feel myself breaking down, no longer able to hold back the emotions and tears and put on the façade that everything was fine. We decided to leave the hospital for awhile and head back to the hotel room for a break. Baby girl was scheduled to have her hearing test screening and her pulse oximetry screening anyway, so we thought this would be a good time to head out and catch our breaths.

Back at the hotel, I allowed myself the ability to cry and release the stress of the situation. At the same time, Nate and I started reaching out to our prayer warriors of our church asking them to pray for us. We needed godly encouragement and strength that only the Holy Spirit could give us. One of my prayer warrior girlfriends suggested that I listen to the song "Yes and Amen" by Housefires. We stayed at the hotel for a few hours. Nathan was so strong. I remember asking him how he could be so calm right now, and I found myself getting mad at him that he wasn't more upset about all that was transpiring, but looking back, that was ridiculous. God allowed him to be exactly the man and husband I needed at that time.

We were able to take a little bit of a nap, and once we awoke, I saw I had a text from Amy asking if we were okay. She said that she noticed we weren't in our room and that the baby was in the nursery, so she took her out of the nursery and put her in her room and said they were having a good ol' time. That took all the calmness I had been working on attaining and put me back into pure panic mode. I texted Amy back letting her know that we were fine and were just resting and on our way back from the hotel. I also asked her if she needed anything while we were out, but I didn't get a response.

Back at the hospital, we walked to Amy's room and saw that she still had baby girl in there. She was holding her like a mother holds her baby, singing to her, and it ripped my heart out. I remember thinking at that very moment that it was over. We weren't going to get her. I saw the love and attachment in Amy's eyes for her, and at that moment, I couldn't have felt less like baby girl's mother.

Amy asked us what we had for dinner, and we told her we had stopped at Popeye's. She looked at us and said, "Hmm…now that you mentioned Popeye's, that does sound really good. Would you mind heading out to get me some?"

I felt like my jaw was on the ground at that moment, and what could Nathan or I do? Amy held the power of our parenthood in the palms of her hands. "No" was not a word allowed in our vocabulary. We had to do whatever she and anyone else asked of us no matter what that was. To say that as adoptive parents you feel exploited throughout the entire process would be an understatement. Each person and entity involved knew that they had the adoptive parents by the tail end, and it seemed to get worse the deeper into the process you traveled.

So we left the hospital, again, and again it was with Amy holding our baby. I began to put up a wall around my heart, fearing this was not going to turn out well for us at all. Once we got to the car, I could see Nathan's emotions had caught up with mine. We, at that time, had to remind ourselves that God is good, and we were going to praise Him no matter the outcome. Throughout our time with Amy, we realized just what an amazing person she was and what an amazing mother she was to her four-year-old son, so if she decided to keep baby girl, we knew that baby girl would be right where God wanted her to be, and she would be okay. We promised God we would praise Him if that happened to be the case, knowing baby girl got to stay with her birth mother and her half-brother. That is not to say we weren't starting to grow the questions in our minds about God's promise to us. We began wondering if God would have allowed us to have traveled 1,900 miles and eight states to go home without a baby, and if so, why?

While driving to and from the hospital that day, we saw the most incredible sunset we had ever seen with the western mountains in the backdrop. I both saw and felt God's beauty in that moment, and I knew He was saying to us that He was still with us and to be still because He was in control. Even so, we made the decision that we would not leave that hospital any longer, not for one minute, until we were discharged either with or without the baby, but we were not going to go without fighting for her.

That night and until eight thirty the following morning, time stood still. The ticking of the clock in our hospital room banged so loudly I swear it had to have been echoing throughout the entire floor. The social worker had said that she would first visit Amy's room, and after about ten minutes, the paperwork should be signed, and she would then come down to our room for us to sign our part.

So 8:30 a.m. came and went, as did 9:00 a.m. and 9:15 a.m. We began pacing the floor and tried with superhuman powers to hold back tears. We could hear our cell phones blowing up with our loved ones wanting an update, but at that moment, we had to ignore them. We had no update, nor did we have the strength to deal with that at that particular moment. Finally, the hospital social worker, not the adoption social worker, stopped to see if we were okay. She saw us pacing and the look of fear in our faces. We told her we were very anxious about what was happening just three doors up, and she said that she would try to get us an update.

In the meantime, we just held baby girl and started praying hard. We also started listening to "Yes and Amen" on YouTube, just as my friend suggested. We tried to find a version from the lead worship director at our church back home, but we couldn't find one. On a sidebar, we later told him this, and he sent us the link he had on Vimeo stating, "Ask and you shall receive."

More time went by. It was now 9:45 a.m., and one of the nurses came down to our room, shutting the door behind her. She asked us if we could give her a brief scenario of the reason behind the adoption as she wanted to get some more insight as to what was going on. We didn't know how much we were able to disclose, so we told her as little as possible. She informed us that Amy was crying uncontrollably, and they were having a hard time getting her to calm down. The nurse then said she had to take baby girl from our room as the pediatrician was there to check on her. *Why did they have to take the baby from our room? Yesterday, the pediatrician visited our room with the baby. Why was this different? What was going on? Should I protest and not let them take the baby?*

Nathan and I were in pure panic mode at this point. That nurse had the exact same look that the technician had during our first miscarriage; the look that she knew something but wasn't able to tell us. We looked at each other and just held each other on the bed. In our minds it was over. They took baby girl away from us, and we would be leaving without her. We weren't even able to hug her or say goodbye. The nurse just wheeled her right out of our room. We were in shock. A few moments later, the hospital social worker came back down to our room and said that Amy was getting ready to sign the paperwork and to just give them another ten minutes or so, and that

Amy wanted the baby in her room for a while to spend some time with her.

At approximately 10:15 a.m., the adoption social worker finally made it to our room. When she first walked in, she had a look of pure concern, as if what she had to say to us was not what she wanted to have to say, but after a few moments, she took out the awaited, signed paperwork, and Nate and I breathed our first deep breath in hours. I still do not know why she had that look about her when she walked into our room or why it took her so long to let us know the outcome of the paperwork, but I can tell you the amount of relief it brought was of seismic proportions. At the exact same time, the pediatrician came into our room and let us know we would be discharged later that morning.

Things were radically changing now, and we could finally begin to see a positive outcome in our future. Amy decided that she didn't want the hospital to be our final goodbye, so she offered to treat us to dinner one evening so that we could all say our goodbyes then. She was hoping her four-year-old son would also be back from staying with his father, so he could meet her as well. We told her we would honor that.

We were discharged on a Wednesday, and our lawyers began working diligently to get our paperwork moving through the court systems. We were told that we had to appear in a temporary custody hearing that following Friday morning. Wednesday night and Thursday, we just sat in awe of our great God. We Skyped our friends and family back home, and we would listen to Christian worship music with her. We also began reading books and praying with our baby girl, giving thanks to the Lord who never breaks His promises.

Once Friday morning came, we all three got into our vehicle and drove the twenty miles to our court hearing. When we arrived, the security guards said they thought we misunderstood the place as they had a big jury case arriving any minute, and so, we must have the wrong place. Again, panic set in. *Now what do we do? Did we mess this up, and are we now going to have to delay going home?*

However, the clerks informed us we were in the correct place and that the judge had agreed to see our case before the big jury case to keep us moving toward home. We realized at that time just how great the state of Utah was in understanding the adoption matter at hand. We later learned that the judge and our representing attorney had both legally adopted children, so these cases held a special place in their hearts. At the same time, we received a phone call alerting us that Utah's ICPC had approved us, and we could begin our journey home. They immediately sent the paperwork to our home state of Pennsylvania, so we could leave Utah, but we could not enter Pennsylvania until they approved. We decided then that we would at least start the trek home, and if necessary, stay in Ohio until Pennsylvania approved us.

I texted Amy to alert her that we would be leaving promptly Saturday morning or possibly Friday night, and if she still wanted to meet, we would have to do lunch after baby girl's forty-eight-hour doctor's appointment.

Amy texted back that she would love to take us to lunch and gave us a spot and a time to meet her after we were done at the pediatrician's. Our doctor there informed us that baby girl looked great and that she was cleared to start the journey home.

Once we arrived at the destination Amy had picked for us, we ordered our lunches and sat down to eat. We placed baby girl on the bench in her car seat beside Amy so that she could have all the time with her that she needed. It didn't make us nervous to do so now that all the paperwork was signed. However, we soon learned that Amy was stalling, in a bad way. Nathan and I had finished our lunches within ten minutes. Two hours later, Amy was still nibbling at her lunch and hadn't even started eating her cake dessert.

Since the birth father wasn't in the picture, Nathan didn't have to deal with the thoughts that go through your mind when the baby's natural parents are holding them. They asked me during our court hearing if I thought I was bonding with baby girl, and of course my answer was yes, but when Amy was holding her, it was so hard to feel as if I was this baby's mother. There was also an awkwardness there now for the first time since we were introduced to Amy. What made the situation even weirder was that Amy's milk had come in, so when she held baby girl, baby girl picked up on that right away and tried to nurse from her. In that moment, I felt disconnected. As if that wasn't enough, bystanders would walk passed and tell Amy what a beautiful baby she had and congratulate her. Rather than explain the situation to every single person, we would all just put on an awkward smile while Amy would thank them.

This happened a few times in the hospital as well. Nate and I talked about this a few times during our stay in Utah—about how we couldn't believe people did not have more empathy for the situation at hand or for any of the parties involved. Once, we were in Amy's hospital room while she was holding baby girl, and a hospital volunteer came in to set up a celebration table with fake champagne, fine silverware and tablecloths, and the whole works. She even had a gift for the parent(s). It just so happened that the hospital social worker was also in the room and explained to the volunteer that this was an adoption case and how we were going to be the child's actual parents, but that didn't stop this woman. She gave us the gift instead and told us congratulations, all the while, she continued setting up the table for Amy. Even the social worker looked uncomfortable with the situation at hand. I remember feeling so sad for Amy. How awkward this must have been for her and uncomfortable.

Another time, actually, it was the exact same day about an hour prior, the breastfeeding consultant came into Amy's room and asked her if this was a good time to begin the nursing proceedings. Amy explained to the woman that she was not breastfeeding and that this information should already be in her chart. The woman glanced back down at the clipboard she was carrying, and when she looked back up, she apologized, saying she did have written down that this was a non-breastfeeding case. That must have been all that she had written down, or at least all that she read, because she continued to ask the reason why Amy chose not to breastfeed. Instead of going into the situation again, Amy just answered that it was her preference.

Nathan and I couldn't help but wonder how these cases were handled when both parties, the birth parents and the adoptive parents, wanted to remain confidential and anonymous to one another. It was obvious that people paid no mind to double check this type of information before spilling out their everyday jargon. I even asked a nurse if they saw a lot of adoption cases, and she said that they saw a few every year at their hospital. We just remember thinking how odd it was that some of the staff cared a great deal and showed great compassion toward the situation while others would just breeze past the information without even a second glance. Perhaps that was more of an issue with hospital policy. Either way, it caused a great deal of awkwardness.

Back to our goodbye lunch, when Amy finally finished her lunch, she asked if it would be okay if she carried baby girl out to the car. My heart was breaking for her, but at the same time, Nate and I were ready to move on from this part of the journey and begin our lives bonding with baby girl. I still stand in awe to this day at the amount of sacrificial love Amy had for baby girl and the bond she was willing to break in order to give this child her best chance. However, after being away from home for almost two weeks now and dealing with intense emotions for the duration of these weeks, we were spent and ready to move forward. We did this the best we could while trying to have sympathy and compassion for Amy, yet we needed to break away from this situation.

We never agreed to an open adoption, and this is the why behind that. We knew it was too awkward for us as her adoptive parents and didn't want anything standing in the way of us being able to bond with baby girl. Amy did make the comment that she wished our paperwork wouldn't have gone through yet as she wanted us to stay until at least Monday night when her son would be back. We began wondering then, as Satan loves to put ideas in our minds, if she was manipulating our paperwork back at the hospital so that we would have to stay, *Was this the reason she was stalling with the social workers?* Whatever the case, we decided we needed to leave Utah as soon as possible to break away and start our lives together as a new family. We did tell Amy we would be willing to do a semi-open adoption and that we would leave it up to her to contact us. We didn't want to be contacting her too often and not allow her the proper healing time, so in order to remain compassionate to her, we told her we would just wait to hear from her when she felt the urge or the need for an update.

Nathan and I decided that we were just too tired Friday night. So on Saturday morning, we left Utah. Nathan stated that he was going to moon Utah the minute we crossed the Utah/Wyoming border. He thought the state was absolutely beautiful, but he wanted to let it know the emotional toll it took on us both. Let's just say that once we hit that border though, we did not stop. Nathan kept his foot pressed on that gas pedal like we were outlawed bandits. Later, when I told our pastor this story, he laughed and thanked Nathan for not mooning the state. He said he didn't need his deacon to be on the newsreel out west for mooning.

We made it to Nebraska on the first day and to Illinois the second day. On the third day, which was now a Monday, we were hoping we would hear from PA's ICPC by the time we got to the Ohio/PA border, which we didn't. I could not understand what the hold up could possibly be, especially given Utah had us approved within hours. I decided to call Harrisburg even though they state not to do so. I was tired of living out of a hotel room, especially now with a newborn. It was time to come home.

After leaving numerous messages via phone and email, I finally got a return phone call from a representative stating they had received our paperwork and that it was held up for missing documentation. However, the representative could not specify to me what was missing. She informed me I had to call another representative who was handling the case. I called that number, and of course, I received another voicemail where I proceeded to leave yet another message. In the meantime, I decided to call our attorney in Utah to see if she had heard anything. She stated that she had not, nor did they send her anything stating they were missing information. She informed us that she had actually reached out to them via email and voice message earlier that morning to check on the status for us with no response.

I proceeded to call the PA office back and left another message with this information. This time, I was more stern on the message. Both my, and my husband's patience, was running out. On top of this, the following day, which was a Tuesday, was a state holiday for Utah. On this day, they observe Pioneer Day, which is their state holiday celebrating family heritage, and all government offices are closed. So, now, we were looking at spending at least another two days in a hotel room with our baby and away from all our friends and family and our two Jack Russell Terriers.

They say that ICPC is for the benefit of the adopted child, but nothing of this benefited her or us. To say Nate and I melted down was an understatement. Our hearts just sank down to the floor. I cannot even describe how tired and over this trip that we were. Each passing day that we were away felt like another week. Our home state of Pennsylvania really let us down. We were embarrassed and disappointed at the way their ICPC department was handled.

I think our attorney could just hear the amount of discouragement in our voices, and she vowed to work on her day off if necessary to try and get us home. There He was. God was there amongst this new roadblock.

Our attorney held true to her word, and she worked that Tuesday in order that we could get the go ahead to come home. What a blessing she was, and the paperwork that was missing? It turned out that Pennsylvania's ICPC didn't like the "wording" on some of the documents, so our attorney had to reword some of them, and we had to resign them—something that took us minutes to complete. I vowed then to write my state representatives about the modernization needs for the ICPC process. As I stated earlier, there were no benefits of this process to our adopted child, nor to us. We felt the process was absolutely ridiculous and in much need of modern standardization, but at least we could now go home.

CHAPTER 7

The Rebuking of the Storm
and the Blessings of Obedience

> He got up, rebuked the wind and said to
> the waves, "Quiet! Be still!" Then the wind
> died down and it was completely calm.
> —Mark 4:39

Crossing the border into Pennsylvania was enlivening. It's funny because I always thought I hated living in Pennsylvania and that I wanted to move to another state, but at that time, Pennsylvania felt like paradise. Nathan said that he wanted to get out of the car and hug the "Welcome to Pennsylvania" sign, but again, he didn't want to lift that foot off the gas pedal. We were finally homebound.

Once home, the blessings of the Lord continued to pour in, so much so that we couldn't keep up with them. Two of our best friends had recently had a baby girl, who at the time was one and a half years old. Weeks before leaving for Utah, they had given us garbage bags upon garbage bags of clothes and supplies that their baby girl had grown out of. Once we got home, we also found they had secretly gone grocery shopping for us so that we would have one less thing to worry about. They checked on our dogs for us for the two weeks we were away, and to this day, they continue to pour out so many blessings too numerous to count.

On top of this, we had come home to a clean house. My sister had house sat for us while we were away during the day, and we had come home to find she had cleaned our house from top to bottom, even shampooing our carpets. Nate's sister and brother-in-law gave us their old nursery furniture, and toys and clothes came pouring in from friends, family, and our church family. Some of the members of the church wanted to throw us a baby shower. However, we felt glutinous doing so as we just had so much. We started having to turn down things, such as the baby shower, because we were bursting at the seams. Not only was baby girl's room full, she started taking over the closets and the shed and laundry room as well.

There is an Old Testament story in the Bible, Exodus chapters 35 and 36, regarding the building of the Tabernacle. God had instructed Moses on what was needed, and all who were willing and whose hearts were moved in the Israelite community, both men and women, brought offerings; so much so, that in chapter 36 verses 5–7, it states that the people had brought more than what would be needed. Moses had to give an order for the people to stop bringing offerings. This is exactly what happened with baby girl. We had so much, and there were just some things that we had to turn down or turn away, although we never turned away gifts for baby girl. Even if we had two or three of something, we never wanted to stop anyone from being a part of God's work and miracle.

Baby girl became a local celebrity fast. News began to spread about what God had done, and people that we hadn't spoken with in years and even old neighbors started coming to the house to see her and to shower her with gifts and love. It was incredible, though it was hard to see the beauty in it at the time because Nate and I were incredibly tired and "jet lagged" so to speak. After traveling over 60 hours and 4,200 miles within a two-week time period, going through the emotional roller coaster of an adoption process, and dealing with the changes, especially in sleep, that comes with a newborn, we actually found we would get irritated at times because there were just so many people all the time. One time, eleven people had stopped throughout the course of one day, and we tried to accommodate everyone, but it started to be at the expense of our sanity.

We really tried hard to fit everyone in so that God's glory could be shown, but we did also have to learn to set boundaries. God showed us that we were stretching ourselves too thin to be of good use. That was parenting lesson number one because it was hard to set boundaries and tell people the dreaded word, "no." Believe me when I say too that it was an unwelcomed word in the vocabulary of many. We had actual family members get upset with us and verbally express it too.

Our first Sunday back to church after the trip was overwhelming in the best way. We couldn't even get out of our car. We got swarmed. Our pastor finally came out to the parking lot to see what the fuss was, and when he saw us, he just smiled. He told everyone to go in and get their morning donuts, but it was so cute. He said it in his way that was so polite, but everyone knew what he was getting at. *Hey, let these people at least get out of their car and into the building.*

God had redeemed us. Psalm 61:1–3 says, "Hear my cry, O God; listen to my prayer. From the ends of the earth I call to you, I call as my heart grows faint; lead me to the rock that is higher than I. For you have been my refuge, a strong tower against the foe." I had come out of this more refined than when I had gone in, and a lot was revealed to me. I knew what and for whom I was willing to fight, and who was willing to fight for me and with me. I learned who my true friends and family were, and that even though I wanted to be in control, I was never in even an ounce of it.

I am really proud of Nathan and I. We withstood the storms and the trials, and we did it in a godly manner, or at least as close as we could get. There were so many times when we wanted to lash out at anybody. It didn't matter who, but we never did. There were so many times where we just thought to ourselves, *It would be easier to give in and quit; throw in the towel; wave the white flag,* but we didn't. We pressed on to take hold of that for which Christ Jesus took hold of us (Phil. 3:12).

In the following months after returning home, it became apparent just how much of a child of God our baby girl really was. She brought so much light to everyone who met her. She also broke down racial barriers and showed those who were willing to look that God still performs miracles, and He still wants to turn the bad that has happened to you into something good—something that can glorify His name.

That is why I wanted to write this novel. I wanted to glorify God's name because this was a dream that Nathan and I pursued that only God could have made come true. I love Walt Disney's saying, *It's fun to do the impossible.* It really is! Going through it was not fun at all, but at the end, seeing something come to fruition that only God could have done is more rewarding than any pain suffered. It is really cool to stand on the other side, out of the boat, and say, "Wow, God. You did this. This is what you wanted for me and needed me to believe in, and it's just like you promised. It is bigger and better than anything I could have ever imagined for myself. Baby girl is just a little peanut, and you have already used her for your purposes and the building of your kingdom." With God, Nathan and I did the impossible, and we lived the impossible.

I implore any of you reading this today that if God has asked you to get into a boat of impossibilities, to get in! There is no greater joy or rush that this world will ever offer you than to be on the other side of the shoreline with God just beaming in all His glory. The sense of fulfillment I got from this journey can never be matched by this world. There is no school lesson that could have ever taught me or given me the knowledge that I am now in possession of, nor the character that I have gained.

CHAPTER 8

Get in the Boat

In order to be successful in our journey, we first had to make sure that this was God's will for our lives, so first things first, be still and listen. Make sure that this is the path God is choosing for you to walk. As Christians, we are told that all glory belongs to our Lord and that there is nothing we can do in our own strength (John 15:5). So it may sound cliché for me to say that this journey would not have been successful without the Lord intervening on all levels, but it is true! There are so many non-guarantees when going through the adoption journey, but because we waited on the Lord to tell us when and where to move, we were able to have peace in all the risks taken.

About four months after we brought baby girl home, we received an email from our adoption attorneys out west. Our adoption would not be finalized until six months, and since the six-month mark was so close to the end of 2018/beginning of 2019, they said that we had the option of filing a motion to have the adoption closed a little early so that it would be complete in 2018 (at approximately the five-month mark). Of course, this would come with a $300–$500 price tag with no guarantees that the judge would allow us to do this. I know, imagine that! No guarantees and no refunds. Shocking. But because we knew this was God moving again, we went for it and got approved to have our hearing in December 2018.

When we heard from the Lord and knew this was His will for us, all the risks kind of dissipated. There are no risks when God is at your back and is the wind in your sails. It's funny, but money stopped being an issue for us because God kept proving to us that it wasn't one for Him. He found a way to meet the price tag every time. Actually, I should rephrase that—He found a way to exceed the price tag every single time. So, before you get into the boat, whatever boat that may be, be sure that God is calling you to it. With this being said, if God does call you to do it, say, "Yes!" Looking back, I think how awfully sad it would have been for Nathan and I had we not said yes to God. Granted, we would have no idea of what we were truly missing out on, but when I look at baby girl, I see just how much of God's blessings we would have lost.

I also think about Mary in the story of Luke 1:26–38. The angel Gabriel had come to tell Mary that she had found favor with God and that she was going to conceive and give birth to a son, and He was to be called Jesus and will be the Son of the Most High. And what was Mary's response to this? In verse 38, she says, "I am the Lord's servant. May your word to me be fulfilled." Mary said yes!! Could you imagine if she would have said no? Mary would have missed out on being part of the greatest story of all time, the greatest event that earth had ever witnessed up to that point in history and would ever witness after. If the word of God is calling you, my prayer is that God will give you the strength to respond as Mary did and as Nathan and I did, "Here I am, Lord."

In the book of Judges chapter 6, we learn of Gideon. At the time of Gideon, Israel was under the oppression of the Midianites. When an angel of the Lord appeared to Gideon, he was working in a secluded place because he was fearful of the Midianites. However, even though he was hiding in fear, God's angel greeted him as a "mighty warrior" (v. 12). I love that God placed stories like this in the Bible because I can only imagine Gideon looking around to find the mighty warrior the angel was talking to. I mean, he couldn't have thought it was himself. He was hiding from the Midianites at the time. However, Gideon was exactly whom God was speaking to and calling mighty.

God wanted to send Gideon to fight the Midianites, but Gideon wanted to be sure that it was truly God calling him to do this. He knew that without God, he would not succeed, so the book goes on to tell how Gideon asked for repeated assurance that God granted him.

Second, have faith. That is easier said than done, but if you know that God is calling you to do the impossible, then you can be sure He is going to call you to greater faith. There were many times when we waited on God to tell us what to do and when to move, but there were also many times that He waited on us to make our moves and exude our faith. I can almost guarantee there are going to be many times while you are traveling with Jesus that He is going to make sure you take faith leaps. It's like that old image of the staircase where only a few steps are showing, but you have to have faith and keep climbing it even though you cannot see the remaining stairs.

This is exactly what God did with us. He would show us one step at a time, and to see the next step, we had to practice faith. Without knowing whether or not we would be a chosen family to adopt, we gave the $16,000, nonrefundable, fee in faith, and it was not easy. Actually, it was quite painful for me. Growing up, my family struggled financially; my father and mother always working to ensure our family needs were met, so I grew up seeing money as a security blanket. Giving up $16,000, especially when it would be with no guarantees, was extremely hard for me to do. That is what God does. He isn't going to test our faith by asking us to do what comes easy to us. He is going to ask us to do something that we find difficult or to give up things that we hold dear. This is one example, but there are many more that I could give. They all lead to the fact that God will wait for you to make a move before He moves. Sometimes, the moves were small, and other times, they were leaps. The interesting thing too is that sometimes, the struggles I had were not struggles at all for Nathan and vice versa. Either way, God wants you to make big faith moves. Neither Nathan nor I knew anything about the adoption process, and honestly, if we would have known the struggles ahead of time, we may not have decided to go for it, and God knew this about us. So, God revealed the path one detail at a time and walked with us one step at a time. People would constantly be asking us questions about the adoption process and what came next. To that, we answered them honestly saying we had no idea. We would get the "yeah, right!" looks, but it was true. We just held on and took it one day at a time. That was truthfully all we could handle. God gives us the strength for each day, not the days ahead of us.

This leads me to another point. God gave you spiritual gifts in order to withstand the journey in which He has called you. I believe in order to go through an adoption process, you cannot be faint of heart, need to be extremely organized, and you kind of have to have a free spirit. Nathan and I have these qualities, and it comes easy to us to kind of "go with the flow." Actually, it's a quality that we have that sort of drives everyone around us crazy. We rarely plan anything. We wake up each day and just fly by the seat of our pants, so to speak.

The organization came in handy with the mounds of paperwork we had to go through, but we also had to have free spirits in the sense of not needing to know what came next. God gave us these gifts specifically for this journey. I remember telling my mother-in-law certain aspects of the adoption process, and distinctly she said there was no way she could ever do it. She needs to know exactly what is going to take place ahead of time for the entire month. God gave you your spiritual gifts for a reason, and He will call you to board your boat according to your gifts. We have a gentleman at church who is a veteran and to whom God gave a love for other veterans and for the PTSD diagnosis that some of these vets go through. He does amazing things for the Lord in this way and uses his gifts to serve. It's ultimately through His divine power that we have everything we need for a godly life through our knowledge of Him who called us by His own glory and goodness (2 Peter 1:3).

One of the biggest things we had to remember to keep doing while we were in the boat was to keep fighting the good fight. Our pastor gave a sermon during Veteran's Day that explained just how we can do this, and I remember thinking during that sermon just how prevalent this was and how we had been doing this without even knowing it. We had to keep fighting even when we felt the journey was too demanding and too hard. 1 Timothy 6:12 tells us to fight the good fight of the faith, and what is wonderful is that if you are a child of God and have the Holy Spirit living inside of you, you don't have to endure this alone. The truth is, you need God in order to withstand these trials and endure the Christian battles we face. Paul knows this and closes his letter to Timothy stating, "Grace be with you all" (1 Tim. 6:21). We could not do this alone or without grace. Paul also challenges us in verse 11 to pursue six things while fighting the good faith fight—righteousness, godliness, faith, love, endurance, and gentleness.

Righteousness meant that we maintained a morally right way of living and thinking. Nathan and I tried to do this by remaining positive no matter what the storm was that we were currently facing. We tried hard not to let our emotions dictate our attitudes. Once, after a Sunday sermon, a fellow deacon of Nathan's commented to us just how wonderful it was that we were always smiling. This meant a lot to us as we tried really hard to continue to choose joy. It was nice that it was noticed. We also had another gentleman say to us that we exuded Jesus's love in our lives. This was the best compliment we could have ever received. This is our life's goal.

Faith: we remained faithful to God by continuing to attend church and remain actively involved in church activities, even though if I am being honest, there were times when we just didn't feel like it. However, we promised the Lord that no matter what the outcome, we would praise Him, so we made it a point to try not to miss any Sunday services or a chance to sing out praises to our God. We also remained faithful in attending our Sunday night prayer service. We wanted to pray over our own situation, of course, but we also wanted to pray over others in the same way they were praying over us. Our pastor always tells us to consider prayer a privilege. We get to pray for one another because Jesus Christ bridged the gap and restored our relationship with our Holy Father if we would only accept His gift. What better privilege could there be than to communicate with our Abba and lift up our fellow brothers and sisters. I also would tell the Lord that no matter what the outcome, I loved Him and always would. God is always faithful to us, and we needed to reciprocate that.

Godliness: We needed to keep our thoughts, behaviors, and beliefs in line with God's word. This was challenging at times, especially when the enemy was whispering words of doubt and discouragement, but we had to remain in God's word and remind ourselves who God is. We also began to cognizantly take an inventory of the things we were saying and shows we were watching on television. These are areas I am still working on with the Lord, but I knew these were things I wanted to be better at, so that if one day the Lord did bless me with a child, I would have better habits and be the godly example our baby deserved. I also wanted to make sure that I was spending time with God each day and worked on a better prayer and meditation life. The fact of the matter is, God will reward obedience, and we wanted to make sure we were being obedient to Him—aligning our behaviors with those of Jesus. Often, I will get quiet with the Lord and ask the Holy Spirit to take an inventory and reveal to me the areas in my life that need aligned with God's word. I highly suggest doing this often. We should all probably do this daily. It's funny because I almost hate asking and doing this because I am afraid of what I may have to repent of and give up, but the funny thing is, my life becomes more fulfilling when I do. It's really amazing how the things I think matter really don't, and giving them up adds incredible peace and joy to my life.

Love: As stated above, we told the Lord that we would love Him no matter how He decided to answer our prayer, but one thing I needed to work on in this department was to love my husband more perfectly and be the wife he needed me to be in these storms and trials. I repented often here and failed my husband more than I care to admit. At times, I would allow my frustrations and emotions to take over my body, and he happened to be the one that was around to take the brunt of it. So, halfway through this journey, I began to stop asking God daily to answer our baby prayer, and instead, started thanking Him for one more day of having Nathan all to myself and for the second chance at love He gave us that we didn't deserve. I also stopped being angry with Nate for being able to handle the situations we faced with extreme grace and calmness. After all, this was the man God was calling him to be, and I needed to remind myself of this and that men and women just handle things differently. I had to stop expecting him to have the exact same effects and emotions that I had. I needed to let us both off the hook actually.

Endurance: This was probably one of the biggest lessons God taught me. I had to learn to endure at every single stage throughout the entire process. There were times when I didn't think I could go on and other times when I just didn't want to. However, quitting is easy. I wanted to live the Christian life God called me to live, and so I knew I had to keep on. Truthfully, because the journey was so difficult, I knew it was God's will. Paul tells Timothy to fight the good fight. He knew it was going to be a fight. Jude verse 3 tells us we have to contend for the faith. One synonym of the word, "contend," is the word, "struggle." Nate and I were going to have to go into battle if we wanted to overcome this and have Christian success. If this would have been something from Satan, it would have been easy. He wasn't, and still isn't, going to try to have me grow my faith or rely more on God. The fact that the journey required a great intensity of endurance proved that it was truly God's path for us. There were many times while going through this when I had to endure just by crying and getting down on my knees and looking up.

The great part is that God doesn't throw us into the battlefield alone. We are soldiers enlisted in the Lord's army (2 Tim. 2:3). Is there any other army in which you would want to be a part? We are soldiers that God has also fortified. He did not send us into this battle ill equipped. "Therefore put on the full armor of God, so that when the day of evil comes, you may be able to stand your ground, and after you have done everything, to stand. Stand firm then, with the belt of truth buckled around your waist, with the breastplate of righteousness in place, and with your feet fitted with the readiness that comes from the gospel of peace. In addition to all this, take up the shield of faith, with which you can extinguish all the flaming arrows of the evil one. Take the helmet of salvation and the sword of the Spirit, which is the word of God" (Eph. 6:13–17).

God had warned me through His Holy Spirit that I was about to go into battle and that it was really important for me to stay rooted in His word. To anyone about to go through an adoption process, I strongly encourage you to get into, and stay into, God's word because it will hold you up when the world and those in it let you down. I say when and not if because there is a lot of heartache to be endured before glory in this process.

Gentleness: I had to remain kind even when my entire body wanted to scream out in rage and disappointment, and God especially required this of me when difficult people surfaced. There were so many times I did not want to remain gentle. There were the times with Amy in the hospital sending us on errands and holding our baby girl while we were gone that I wanted to scream out in anguish, but the Lord would gently remind me that this really wasn't a big request, especially from someone willing to give me their child. I had to remain gentle with the CYS agents even when I didn't think or feel as if they had the child's best interest at heart. I also wanted to scream at our ICPC representatives in our home state that seemed to literally sit on our paperwork. God had to show me that I could only see it from my own viewpoint and could not see the entire picture. I also had to be reminded that it was not my place to judge anyone. I needed to humble myself and replace myself below God where I belonged.

After the adoption, I continued to pray over Amy, and God began to show me just how much of a sacrifice she had made. I remained so blind and caught up in my own struggles that I wasn't seeing this from her side as much as I should have. I only made it six weeks and then four weeks into my pregnancies, and I had a connection with those babies. Amy had a full-term pregnancy where she got to see the baby on the ultrasound pictures, hear the baby's heartbeat, and feel her moving inside of her womb. There was a strong bond there. On top of that, Amy only really knew Nathan and I for about four months, and even that was sporadic. We spoke mostly over text messages and emails and once over Skype. It wasn't until we traveled out west that she got to meet us in person, and yet, she was willing to trust us enough with this life growing inside of her and hope we were the people she thought we were. What a whirlwind of emotions she must have gone through from the start.

Stop fearing the what-ifs and start living in awe of God's greatness. I am someone who struggles daily with the sin of anxiety, but I wanted to stop living this way. I wanted to leave this world with some sort of legacy—leave it better because I was a part of it and make some sort of impact, if only a small one. There is a famous quote from missionary C.T. Studd that states, "Only one life, 'twill soon be past, only what's done for Christ will last." I want to live in and for the glory of God, and that is my prayer for you as well. I hope my story, God's testimony, has brought you encouragement to sail the seas God is calling you to navigate whether that is an adoption journey or some other journey. Make the dash between your gravestone count—the one that signifies the date you were born and the date of your passing.

I never expected God to do something this significant with my life. In fact, I never felt worthy of Him moving in my life at all. I just started asking God to show me His will for me, and that is when the boat appeared on the shoreline of my life. The boat was on the edge of the shore, bobbing back and forth between the waves. Jesus was standing in the middle of it with an outstretched hand to help me get in. I looked passed Jesus, and all I could see was water. I could not see any other stretch of land in sight. The Holy Spirit gently reminded me not to look passed Jesus, but to look at Him, always, and so, I looked back to Jesus, took His hand, and got into the boat. On the other side, God gave purpose to my heartache and fulfillment to my dreams. God alone deserves all the praise.

What is truly amazing now too is that I have had friends and family, calling me and asking me to encourage them through miscarriages they have suffered. I love that God can use me in this manner. I can actually empathize with them and know on a deeper level their anguish and hurt. God can use us right where we are and use those awful situations for His ultimate glory. I still stand in awe of this fact.

There has probably been a time in your life when you have heard about Jesus and what He has done throughout the Bible. I tell you though, it is not enough to just know about Jesus. We have a part to do too. Jesus says in Revelation 3:20, "I stand at the door and knock. If anyone hears my voice and opens the door, I will come in and eat with that person, and they with me." He also says in Matthew 7:7–8, "Ask and it will be given to you; seek and you will find; knock and the door will be opened to you. For everyone who asks receives; the one who seeks finds; and to the one who knocks, the door will be opened."

The fact is, Jesus has already done His part for us. He left heaven to become a man and walk the earth, die a sinner's death even though He never sinned, was crucified, buried, and resurrected to pay for yours and my sins, so that we may be reconnected with our Heavenly Father and have the Holy Spirit living inside us. We are then also guaranteed to spend eternity in heaven with Him. However, we still have to do our part. Jesus knocks at the door, but we have to open it. We can do this by acknowledging that He is the Son of God, repenting of our sins, and living a life sold out to Christ.

This is the part of Christianity I never got before until I had heard my fellow coworkers talking about salvation. I thought it was enough to know about Jesus and to attend church once in a while, mainly on holidays. I actually thought that would get me into heaven, that and my good works, which the Bible tells us is not truth. There is no amount of good works that can pay for your sin and brokenness. But this is what the Bible is all about. It shows us that Jesus was enough and paid our sin debt, and we can begin to enjoy a restored fellowship with Him and our Heavenly Father if we would only acknowledge this and repent and start living for Him. If you are ready to begin to follow Jesus as your Lord and Savior, I urge you to read the example of a salvation prayer below:

> Dear Lord Jesus,
>
> I admit that I am a sinner, and I am sorry for my sins. Please forgive me. I acknowledge that you are the Son of God and that you died on the cross, shedding your blood for the payment of my sins, and you arose from the grave, conquering death. I need you, Jesus, and I ask you to come and take your rightful place as leader in my life. Help me to live a life sold out to you. Be my savior. Be my Lord. It's in your mighty name I pray. Amen.

If you have just prayed this prayer, I say to you, congratulations and welcome to the kingdom. I also encourage you to speak to your pastor or others you know that are following Jesus so that you can connect and have this mutual encouragement and support. The Bible tells us in Luke 15:10, "In the same way, I tell you, there is rejoicing in the presence of the angels of God over one sinner who repents." How cool to know that if you just prayed the prayer of salvation, angels are rejoicing for you in the presence of God!

If you have never taken a leap to achieve a God-sized dream, do it! Watch God unfold the miracles of your dream, and then you can stand in awe of just how big your God is. If you see Jesus right now on that boat with His hands outstretched, don't look passed Him or walk away. Grab His hand and get in the boat with your Savior, and then watch the invincible, immortal, unpredictable, and unstoppable God make your life count!

> Journal Entry: June 29, 2016
> God is speaking to me about this adoption and reaffirming that it is His will for us and for the child He has chosen.
> I hear you, God. Thank you, and please keep talking to me through this.
> I heard something today that said excitement is the Holy Spirit confirming God is pleased with what you are doing.
> Jesus, we are doing this to serve you!

> Journal Entry: July 2, 2016
> Jesus can heal *every* hurt (Isa. 61).
> More adoption paperwork filled out today. There is so much! But, through Christ, we will press through, even though it is extremely overwhelming at times.

Journal Entry: Monday, July 18, 2016

Home study for the adoption was done on Friday. Our caseworker was really sweet and hopeful that all will go smoothly for us.

This has been a wonderful and also an eye-opening experience so far. We have had to do trainings online regarding the effects fostering has on children. It's really heartbreaking. I hope God can use us in big ways and hopefully choose us to care for one of His own!

Journal Entry: November 1, 2016

The adoption process is really wild and wearisome. It is really hard to know which agency to use and which doors to open. We are really seeking the Lord's guidance on this.

It's almost the holiday season, and I really feel a void at this time of year. The quietness is deafening. Christmas just doesn't feel right to me now, as if I am missing someone or something.

Journal Entry: November 14, 2016

Adoption Stuff: God's Interventions

God has been shutting the door on the India adoption, and we decided to go another route. There were just too many paperwork inconsistencies, it was hard to get in touch with the agents there, and they scarcely stay in touch with us.

On top of that, a news story today said that India and Pakistan may be going to war. God is shutting this door.

Called CYS regarding Mary's two great-nephews again. The CYS agent spoke down to me. She said I probably had the wrong home study done anyway, that I probably didn't do the proper trainings, and that their fourteen-year old sister may want to be adopted with them. She assured me she would send my info on to their caseworker but not to expect a response!

Got accepted into another adoption agency, and it has been amazing so far! It reminds me that when God sees us doing our part, developing what He has given us, then He will do His part and open doors that no man can shut (Isa. 22:22; Rev. 3:8).

Journal Entry: December 19, 2016

A check came in the mail on Saturday. Apparently, there was a Wal-Mart settlement, and since I worked one day there a long time ago, I was part of the settlement. I ended up getting $467.00. God is so funny! He truly comes through in weird/miraculous ways.

We can hopefully save that for the adoption or for whatever God places on our hearts.

"Again, truly I tell you that if two of you on earth agree about anything they ask for, it will be done for them by my Father in heaven" (Matt. 18:19).

God is going to help me and Nate adopt!!!

Also, our adoption profile is finally up and running on the agency's website. We sent it on to our pastor to read, and this was the response we received back, "Wow. That was awesome to read. Brought me to tears. Thanks for allowing me to read it. As always, I am praying fervently for you. I look forward to the day we see the Lord's answer, and we get to partner with you guys. We love you guys!"

Journal Entry: February 14, 2017

Nate and I suffered another miscarriage this week. We found out last Tuesday that we were pregnant but remained "cautiously optimistic."

Over the weekend, I started having severe abdominal pain and bleeding. The local OB-GYN office was once again a struggle to deal with.

I find that people say the strangest things too. One lady told me that if I was good, then God would bless me with a child.

Journal Entry: April 19, 2017

I am struggling with the fact that some-times, it feels as if Nate isn't grieving over the loss of our babies, at least not in the way that I am. This makes me feel secluded and alone. I know deep down that it isn't true and that Nate is grieving and that men just handle it differently. Perhaps Nate is just trying to be the strong one or is trying to find a way to fix it.

Journal Entry: April 26, 2017

Received a phone call yesterday from our pastor's wife. She said that for some reason, I was weighing on her heart, and she was having a hard time sleeping over thoughts of me. We had kept our second miscarriage a secret, or at least we only told our families. I felt this was God telling me that I needed to let her know about it, so I told her.

She scolded me over not allowing them to share our pain and struggles and not allowing them to be there for us. How amazing is God to allow us to have this type of support! Her daughter also gave me the names and phone numbers of some doctors in the city to look into.

Journal Entry: May 14, 2017
"Mother's Day"
This is always an extremely hard day for me now. Nathan's cousin texted him this morning with the text reading, "Happy Mother's Day." A second text came through that read, "Ooops, LOL! That was supposed to go to your sister."

All I could do was shut my eyes and pray. The pains that were brought to my heart and the sickness in my stomach could not even be described. I tried to find contentment in this day, and I did so by knowing I still had my mother with me. I didn't cry all day!

Journal Entry: May 24, 2017
"Standing in the gap"
We had dinner with our pastor and his wife last night at a local Applebee's Restaurant. There, they told us how they were in Orlando last week and attended church. It was the church's Mother's Day Saturday night service, and they said the pastor had added a part in his sermon for those who were trying to have children but couldn't. He then asked if anyone wanted to come up in the gap and pray for themselves or anyone else they knew trying to have children. Our pastor and his wife went into the gap to pray for us! My heart explodes with deep love for them. There is no way we get through this without their support!!!

Journal Entry: Tuesday, July 18, 2017
Pretty sure I heard the Lord call out to me today to tell me to start building the nursery

and take the first step. I had a dream last week as well that we were going to get a phone call in November for triplets, all girls, all their names starting with the letter "A."

Journal Entry: December 15, 2017

Dear God,

I am in a really good, peaceful, happy place right now, totally content in you and all your good works and gifts. I know each day brings its own trials, but knowing there is nowhere I could go where you wouldn't be with me is comforting. I still know that I need to get deeper in your word and spend more quiet time with you, Abba, as well as let go of my pride issues that distance me from you. There were times in my past where I felt you may have forsaken me, but I know that to not be true (Ps. 39)!

—Sheen

Journal Entry: January 12, 2018

Mary's great-nephews are back up for adoption. I have tried calling CYS for days and finally received a call back. They informed me that, again, these boys are not going up for adoption yet and that they are giving the parents another three months, a sort of make or break time for them.

On top of that, they will need a family that can take in their now fifteen-year-old sister. Nathan and I discussed this, and we know that right now we cannot take her in too.

God shut this door and answered this prayer, even though He said no.

Journal Entry: January 15, 2018

Received an email from our home study caseworker a few days ago with a picture of a little girl with special needs in need of a home. However, by the time we got back to the email, she had already been placed. Another door closed and an answered prayer from the Lord.

I get such mixed emotions with these. On the one hand, I am so excited that these children find their homes, yet on the other hand, we are sad that it isn't with us. Just getting pictures creates a bond sometimes.

Journal Entry: March 29, 2018

Received a long-awaited phone call from our agency that we have a potential birth mom. We started texting her tonight. She is pregnant with a baby girl due approximately toward the end of July. My first phone call was to Nate to tell him. He was still at work, so I had to call him there. He actually thought I was joking at first.

My second phone call was to our pastor and his wife!

Journal Entry: March 31, 2018

Had a great phone interview with Amy. She actually said over the phone that the baby was ours; however, our agency tells us to take that with a grain of salt.

Journal Entry: April 2, 2018

We learned today that Amy called our agency and said that before she decided, she wanted to speak with us some more.

We texted her more and more over the phone, and she had questions for us that we tried to answer. It's difficult to know just how much to communicate. We want to get as much information as possible while not pushing too much.

Journal Entry: April 6, 2018
  Got an official e-mail from Amy asking if we would be the adoptive parents. She also sent us over ultrasound pictures and videos.
  My best friend said she was already planning my shower! My family is texting with excitement constantly.

Dear God,
  Your timing is amazing! Why do I doubt? Praise be to you, my King. Thank you God for giving me constant grace and mercy that I don't deserve.

—Sheen

Journal Entry: May 9, 2018

Adoption Updates:
- Skype'd Amy Sunday about a birthing plan. Hoping to get induced to give us a clearer date. She said if we came out a few days early, she could show us around.
- We got our lawyer lined up
- Amy gave us an idea about making our own voice recordings for the baby. She said she would put the recording on her belly and let the baby listen so that the baby would recognize our voices.
- Our prayer group and warriors continue to pray for us
- Our pastor wants to help us with our travel expenses.

- We did have to let our family know we didn't want them to travel with us. We could tell this was a let down for them; however, we wanted this to be an intimate time that we had together, just Nate and I, with our new baby girl. Plus, we didn't want to overwhelm Amy.
- Baby Girl's nursery is full already from the many blessings of our friends and family. It's amazing to see how God can use those around us to bless us. We cannot out give God!

The adoption process has helped me to understand why God gave me gifts of love and organization.

Journal Entry: June 1, 2018
Amy continues to be amazing as are all those that surround us. We got more ultrasound pics of our baby girl today!
I am struggling a little with the stress of everything. God says to stay calm and that He is fighting all my battles!

Journal Entry: June 8, 2018
We have gotten three offers now for baby showers! Plus, friends of ours at church have offered to have their sister do our newborn pics. We already have something set up for that, so we asked if they would be willing to do baby girl's Christmas pics, and they said that would be amazing. The blessings continue to pour in! We are overwhelmed and in awe of the amount and just how many people are excited for this baby!

June 8 was my last journal entry. The rest, from the beginning of the journey until about four months post-adoption, I began writing the pages you are now reading. I hope this look into my personal thoughts and feelings will help give you the empathy you need in your own journey.

BIBLIOGRAPHY

Batterson, Mark. *Chase The Lion: If Your Dream Doesn't Scare You, It's Too Small.* Colorado Springs: Multnomah, 2016.

Poling, Judson and Bill Perkins. *NIV The Journey Bible.* Grand Rapids: Zondervan, 2014.

Saake, Jennifer. *Hannah's Hope: Seeking God's Heart in the Midst of Infertility, Miscarriage, and Adoption Loss.* Colorado Springs : NavPress, 2005.

ABOUT THE AUTHOR

Sheena Rock lives in a small town in Western Pennsylvania with her husband, Nathan, and their little girl. She and Nathan were high school sweethearts who later eloped in the Bahamas. She holds an associate degree in medical office administration and later sought certification as a medical coder, but she now thrives as a stay-at-home mother and author. In her spare time, she enjoys cycling, yoga, antiquing, gardening, and walking her two Jack Russell Terriers. She is also an avid participant at her church and loves the Lord.